KU-790-883

CHE GUEVARA AND THE CUBAN REVOLUTION
Mike Gonzalez

BOOKMARKS

London and Sydney

For Rachel,
Anna
and Dominic

Mike Gonzalez is a senior lecturer in Hispanic Studies at Glasgow University. He has written widely on Latin American literature and culture, and on the politics of contemporary Latin America—in particular on Cuba, Nicaragua and Chile. He is on the editorial board of International Socialism journal and is a member of the Socialist Worker Platform within the Scottish Socialist Party. He is also a regular broadcaster, particularly on radio, and has been involved in a range of theatre projects.

Che Guevara and the Cuban Revolution – Mike Gonzalez
First published 2004
Bookmarks Publications Ltd, c/o 1 Bloomsbury Street,
London WC1B 3QE
Bookmarks, PO Box A338, Sydney South, NSW 2000, Australia
Copyright © Bookmarks Publications Ltd

ISBN 1 898876 45 2

Printed by Cambridge Printing

| Contents

1 **The face in the crowd** | 1

2 **Rediscovering the man** | 7

3 **Travelling the highways,
searching the horizon** | 19

4 **The banana republic** | 27

5 **The Cuban dimension** | 37

6 **82 men and a boat** | 51

7 **La sierra y el llano:
the mountain and the plain** | 61

8 **The short march to Havana** | 75

9 **Guerrillas in power** | 91

10 **Spreading the revolution** | 105

11 **The measures taken** | 119

12 **The 13 days – and after** | 133

13 **Neither marriage nor divorce** | 143

14 **A final journey** | 157

15 **Death and resurrection** | 169

Notes | 175

Watching the 100,000 strong anti-capitalist demonstration in Brussels
Jess Hurd www.reportdigital.co.uk

**Amargit Singh using his CWU card vote at TUC
conference 2002, Blackpool**   Jess Hurd www.reportdigital.co.uk

Residents drop anti-war banners from windows at the European Social Forum in Florence, November 2002

Jess Hurd www.reportdigital.co.uk

May Day demonstration in Revolution Square, Cuba, 1988

Julio Etchart www.julioetchart.com

1 | The face in the crowd

The landless workers of Brazil carry two images when they occupy unused land. One is the leader of the rural community of Canudos, which fought the state in the 1890s. The other is Che Guevara. In Caracas, in Buenos Aires, in Bolivia and in El Salvador young people taking on the police in protests against global capital cover their faces with scarves that the carry the image of Che. In Europe demonstrators wear red T-shirts with the face of Guevara imprinted across their chest.

Ernesto 'Che' Guevara died young. This Argentine doctor who left his country and his career to join the Cuban Revolution was murdered in a Bolivian mountain village while he lay wounded on a bare table. It was October 1967, and Ernesto Guevara was not yet 40 years old.

In Cuba itself, where Che was a charismatic and powerful leader of the revolution of 1959, his face picked out in neon lights decorates the several floors of a public building in Revolution Square in Havana. And on posters and hoardings Che's image sits besides exhortations to support the Cuban government. As you walk around the cities of Cuba it is Che's face that fills the public spaces rather than the man who has dominated Cuban political life ever since the revolution – Fidel Castro.

There is now an entirely new generation who instantly recognise the deep eyes and wispy beard of Guevara, who wear the T-shirt and buy the enormous variety of consumer goods that carry that famous image. Yet in most cases they have very little knowledge and no memory of the Cuban Revolution. In fact the details of Guevara's life are not well known. Yet there seems to be some tacit agreement that the face has a symbolic power and a meaning that everyone understands and can acknowledge.

The groups of musicians that circulate around the tourist resorts in Havana have one song in common – Carlos Puebla's hymn to Che called 'Hasta Siempre' ('Until Forever'):

> Aquí se queda la clara, la entrañable transparencia,
> De tu querida presencia, comandante Che Guevara
> (You left behind the clear, heart-warming visibility
> Of your dear presence, comandante Che Guevara)

The word hymn seems appropriate. This, and the hundreds of other songs and poems that commemorate Guevara, seem to share a language of resurrection, of a dead martyr who will rise again. The most famous photograph of all – bare torso, drawn features, deep black eyes and a sparse beard – was taken shortly before his death. Reproduced a thousand times since then, it seems each time to become more and more like one of a series of familiar tableaux of the dying Christ.

That curious transformation sets in sharp relief one

aspect of Guevara – the man becomes legend, and his image is changed into a representation of a feeling, a spirit. It is that spirit of revolution, of a kind of crusading commitment and fervour, that a new generation has taken from the pictures of the dead revolutionary. In a way Che's life, his historical experience, his real actions, have faded into the background – although at some level most people know of Che's relationship with Cuba.

In an era of corrupt politicians, when very few people have any faith left in their leaders and representatives – or indeed in an electoral process that can bring George Bush to power without a majority – integrity and dedication become important values. Look at the heroes of the anti-capitalist movement – Malcolm X, Martin Luther King, Che. What they have in common is their selflessness, their dedication, their unstinting commitment to a cause. All three died as young men, and all are preserved in the popular memory as youthful, idealistic and unstained.

In 1989 the Berlin Wall was brought down and exposed the terrible reality of the countries of Eastern Europe which had described themselves, until that point at least, as 'socialist'. Hundreds of thousands of progressive people had in the past equated these societies with progress towards socialism. After all, these societies claimed they had no private owners of capital, that the state governed in the name of the whole of society, that their people were free and enjoyed a high standard of living and a just distribution of wealth. Some socialists had always insisted that these were corrupt caricatures of socialism with a ruling class that defended its interests above those of the majority. These were not socialist countries with some shortcomings, they said, but societies *organised* around the interests, needs and purposes of a minority who controlled the state.[1]

Yet when the wall came down what lay exposed to public view was in some ways even worse than we had imagined. Small bureaucracies had terrorised their populations, grown rich at their expense, and deprived them of any control over their own lives. How could this have anything to do with a vision of change rooted in the idea of freedom and collective power? What had the Romanian orphans, the Stasi police state of East Germany or the persecution of the Chechens and other minorities in common with that socialist vision?

The problem was that all these acts had been committed by people who described themselves as socialists, and sometimes even as revolutionaries.

Out of this fog of confusion and disappointment, the image of Che Guevara re-emerged across the world, rediscovered by another generation. The extraordinary Zapatista rebels of southern Mexico wore their characteristic red scarves imprinted with his face when they announced their insurrection against global capital in 1994.[2] The urban rioters of Caracas in 1989 waved placards carrying his image, as did the young Italians demonstrating against the first Berlusconi government five years later.

This symbolic face has a real power, a charge of anger and conviction that belongs to those who carry the image as much as to its origins. It represents a rage against an imperialism whose mask has fallen once again in Iraq and Palestine to expose the ruthless face beneath. It represents a revolutionary yearning, too, for a world without injustice, dispossession or inequality.

At the same time, it represents an absence, a sign of questions still unanswered and contradictions unresolved. How will this other world be fashioned – this 'better world' whose possibility, and urgency, has been the theme of the social forums that have come to define the resistance to global capital?

In this search for answers to urgent, historic questions, the new anti-capitalist movement turns only with suspicion to those experiences of the past so tarnished by corruption and hypocrisy. Somehow the authentic revolutionary tradition that has always insisted that socialism and freedom are indivisible, that workers' power can only be exercised by the workers themselves and not by others on their behalf, has been half-buried in the rubble, too.

The symbolism of Che – the beret, the star and the red scarf – is, if you listen carefully, a call for a different revolutionary tradition, for a different project for transforming society. That project already has its own general character – it is generous, honest, selfless and romantic. And it is youthful. Beyond that, there remain many questions still unanswered as our movement seeks its way forward.

In this open and urgent debate about the kind of future we want to build, Che Guevara can deliver some practical, political responses – once we probe beyond the symbol to the life and the real political history.

Che Guevara, 1960   Osvaldo Salas

2 | Rediscovering the man

Ernesto Guevara was born on 14 May 1928 in Argentina. Before he was two, the country would enter a period of military rule after 15 years of a liberal republic presided over by President Hipólito Yrigoyen. His presidency had marked a profound change in Argentine society, a change that began in the 1880s. Then, Argentina became the meat-exporting economy which fed Europe and received its goods in exchange. But goods were not all that travelled back and forth across the Atlantic. So did people – the poor farmers and unemployed workers of northern Italy, Spain and Germany, drawn by the cheap travel and the promise of prosperity that Argentina offered to the new immigrants.

The great port city of Buenos Aires grew rich on foreign trade, but the immigrants were not welcomed into the expanding city with its proud avenues built in imitation of Paris. They were kept close to the docks, in the crowded, brightly painted wooden houses of the ghetto of La Boca. There they spoke the odd hybrid language called *lunfardo*, mixing Italian and Spanish, and danced the tango – the sensual dance music played enticingly by the brothel bands in this strange world of young working-class men without women.

As Buenos Aires changed and developed, the great slaughterhouses and packing plants became the heart of the growing working-class movement. Anarchist and social-ist ideas flourished among the new workers – and it was no accident that so many of their leaders were recent Euro-pean immigrants. By 1916 the increasing militancy of work-ers paralleled the rising discontent of an urban middle and lower middle class still largely excluded from political life, for Argentine society was still dominated by the old landowning classes living in the grand, ornate mansions of the Belgrano district.

In that year, when full male suffrage was introduced, it was Yrigoyen's Radical Party which became the govern-ment. It introduced social security and other measures, but beyond government other forces were gathering. The University Reform movement of 1918, which began in the city of Córdoba, spread through the continent, demanding a democratic higher education and a change in what was taught. A new education should reflect the reality of a Latin America seeking new directions, bent on building independent nation-states, and rewriting its own history. A year later the working class occupied the centre of the his-torical stage in the great strike movement of 1919.

By the time that Che was born the radical hopes of those early years were slipping away, and Yrigoyen fre-quently turned against his working-class support in an effort to assuage the wealthy. By 1930 the old interests felt strong enough to respond. The real purposes of the mili-tary coup of that year were revealed soon enough, when in 1933 the new regime signed a trade agreement with

Britain – the Roca-Runciman Pact – which restored the old economic powers. For the working class this was a clear defeat.

Guevara's parents belonged to the provincial middle class. Guevara himself acknowledged that his family came from a cattle-raising oligarchy with distant links to Ireland on the one side and the ruling Spanish colonial elite on the other. Ernesto's father, a not very successful businessman, moved his family from the Misiones region on the border with Paraguay to Buenos Aires to Rosario in pursuit of one misguided project or another. Frustration seems to have defined the atmosphere in the family home as each project came to grief.

At an early age the young Ernesto contracted asthma. The city of Buenos Aires was intolerable for the young boy, so his family moved first to the city of Córdoba and from there to Altagracia, in the province of which it was the capital.

Asthma dogged and shaped Guevara's early life. His school attendance was erratic and he was for the most part educated by his mother, a determined woman with a leaning towards risk-taking. How far his asthma influenced his character is disputed – though one biographer (Castañeda) insists that it was fundamental. What is clear from the testimony of childhood friends and family members is that he was stubborn and sometimes reckless, insisting on playing rugby even if his play was constantly interrupted by grabs for his inhaler:

> The character traits that later acquired legendary dimension in the adult Guevara were already present in the boy. His physical fearlessness, inclination to lead others, stubbornness, competitive spirit and self-discipline – all were clearly manifest in the young 'Guevarita' of Altagracia.[3]

There is very little to suggest that the young Ernesto was particularly concerned with politics at this stage in his life. He said as much himself:

> I wasn't concerned about social questions in my adolescence and I never took part in any student struggles or political activities in Argentina.[4]

He seems to have been much more fascinated by the adventure stories of Jules Verne and others – and by the ordinary concerns of a growing middle-class youngster with something to prove about his physical capacities and his ability to keep pace with his fitter contemporaries. Rugby, which fascinated him, was more than a game: it was the arena in which young Argentine men of the elite rehearsed their journey into masculinity.

While his family were not noticeably politically active, they were clearly aware of events in the world. His mother ran a Bohemian household which often gave shelter to writers and artists as well as visitors like the family of Spanish Republican refugees who arrived in the house late in 1937. His father was much more directly involved in an organisation collecting aid and support for the besieged Spanish Republic. Although their political allegiances were to the Liberal party, the Guevaras were anti-fascist and as concerned as hundreds of thousands of others across the world that a victory for fascism in Spain would be a disaster for democracy.

But while Ernesto (barely ten years old) must have been aware of the reasons for the arrival of these strangers from Spain, there is nothing to suggest that he was some kind of precocious revolutionary. More important, perhaps, than these directly political questions is the matter of the social class to which the family belonged.

Although his father's businesses tended towards brief prosperity followed by failure, Ernesto's was a middle-class family with some claims to a rather more illustrious ancestry in Spain and Ireland. In the capital his relatives were comfortably off, though his own home was less secure and prone to lean times. Nevertheless, Che never made any claims to a childhood of want. It was not personal experience of privation that would make of him the revolutionary he became.

Yet in some very important ways his adolescent world did form him politically as well as psychologically. Whether or not he was conscious of politics – and the evidence is that he was not particularly interested – events outside himself shaped the young Che. As an Argentine, of course, the Second World War was not the shaping experience it was for young Europeans. But its echoes influenced internal events nevertheless.

Ernesto's father, still active in anti-fascist circles, was convinced that Argentina was the site for much pro-Nazi activity among some of those in its German communities.[5] There was also much barely concealed sympathy for the Axis among sections of the Argentine military, particularly those who had visited Mussolini's Italy during the 1930s, like Juan Domingo Perón. In his memoirs, Guevara's father describes some of the cloak and dagger activities in pursuit of secret Nazi cells in Córdoba province.[6] He claims for his son a kind of nascent anti-fascist consciousness – but Ernesto's friends simply acknowledge that Hitler and Mussolini would occasionally figure in the games of soldiers that they played.

It may be that the military government in power in Argentina at the outbreak of the Second World War was more concerned about the fate of the European markets for its beef and wheat. Britain, historically its most important customer, was now subject to German shipping activity in the South Atlantic; the rest of Europe was inaccessible because of Allied blockades, and the United States was unresponsive to the Argentine search for new markets. The military government of Castillo which came to power in 1940 showed some sympathy for the Hitler-Mussolini Axis.[7] But there were also ideological reasons why an authoritarian nationalist government would feel neutral towards the old imperial power, Britain. The protection of domestic interests overrode any other consideration. Indeed war, for a country whose main exports – meat and wheat – drove the competing armies, was a commercial opportunity.

In 1943, as Ernesto's father continued his erratic course as an unremarkable businessman, the family moved to the city of Córdoba. Meanwhile in the capital, Buenos Aires, the political scene was changing. Castillo had nominated as his successor a man known to have connections with British capital. There was a strong suspicion that he would declare for the Allies and enter the war, a suspicion held, for example, by a small group of nationalist army officers – the GOU – whose hostility to the old imperial power was matched by admiration for Mussolini's Italy. Just after the Guevaras moved to Córdoba, Castillo was overthrown by a military coup led by an army faction influenced by the GOU.

A state of emergency was declared, all political activity was suspended and student protests were crushed. Although he was accidentally involved in one street clash with police, Ernesto was largely unconcerned (although not necessarily unaffected) by these changes. However, his close friend Alberto Granado was arrested during the demonstration and jailed.

Given Che's later history, it should come as no surprise that the discovery of early signs of his political awareness has become a minor industry. The evidence, however, suggests a young man shaped by his class background. The much-repeated story of his attempt to rescue a crippled beggar from stone-throwing kids testifies to a generous spirit. The beggar's well-attested reaction – turning on the young man and cursing him – might tell us how clearly he bore the marks of his class. This does not undermine Che's political development. On the contrary, it underlines how significant a leap of consciousness it was that he should eventually become a revolutionary.

A few months before the end of the war, early in 1945, the Argentine government declared for the Allies – presumably having seen which way the wind was blowing. The fact that Argentina was a haven for many escaping Nazi leaders, however, suggests that the sympathies of those in power were less sincerely anti-fascist. But in the intervening two years it was the small group of younger nationalist officers led by Juan Domingo Perón who were shaping events from the shadows. When his patron at the war ministry became vice-president Perón asked to be moved to the Secretariat of Labour. It was a very clever decision. In his time there Perón transformed the secretariat into a powerful ministry from which he could build a mass base of support for his future political ambitions. Briefly jailed in October 1945 on an island prison in the River Plate, Perón was freed after mass demonstrations of workers demanded his release. He returned to Buenos Aires and addressed the crowds from the balcony of the presidential palace – the Casa Rosada or Pink House. Less than a year later Perón became president of Argentina.

Millions of words have been written in an attempt to define and pin down the politics of Juan Domingo Perón. If many attempts to analyse Peronism are inconclusive, that is because the politics of Juan Perón were as elusive and contradictory as the character of his most famous representative – his wife Evita.[8] Perón was a class populist, claiming to speak for several different social sectors and articulating the demands of each in a completely opportunistic way. What is undeniable is that the great demonstrations that demanded his release from prison and later met him in the capital's central square, the Plaza de Mayo, were overwhelmingly working class (Che himself was probably present by coincidence at the great October demonstration). But it was not all the working class. Perón's base of support was a layer of newly arrived workers, recent immigrants from the countryside or the smaller provincial towns, who had gravitated towards the capital in search of work in its expanding industries. They were largely ununionised, despite the traditional strength of Argentina's trade union movement.

Evita came from the same world as they, spoke with their accent, and could claim to understand their needs. Perón allowed her to speak on his behalf – and in doing so guaranteed the allegiance of this group who were called the 'shirtless ones' – the *descamisados*. They were Perón's mass base. As minister of labour, Perón introduced a number of welfare measures which benefited them. And it was true that Perón enjoyed support from other sections – business groups opposed to British influence and some right wing nationalists, among others. Opposing him in the 1946 presidential elections was another equally broad and confusing coalition, the Democratic Union, which enjoyed support from other sections of business as well as socialists and Communists.

From the point of view of the Argentine Communist Party, Perón had used his stint at the labour ministry to build new organisations to challenge the traditional trade unions, many of which were led by Communists. Equally, the allegiance of the Communists to the Soviet Union and its interests internationally led them to see Perón's overt support for the German-Italian Axis during the war as the key question. So they denounced Perón persistently as a covert Nazi.[9] Now, while Perón's wartime vacillations might have encouraged such a view, for hundreds of thousands of workers he was a defender of workers' interests who on several occasions had intervened in industrial disputes to support workers against their employers. There was no doubt that he did so for pragmatic reasons, tying the unions to the state and transforming them into political instruments for his own use. When he turned against the old trade unions in the late 1940s, that influence became a key weapon – and would remain so even after his overthrow ten years later.

For Guevara's parents, however, Perón was the devil incarnate. His mother's political sympathies and connections, such as they were, were with the Communist Party. His father was involved with Acción Argentina, a broad anti-fascist organisation. For the Communists, the result of their hostility to Perón was that within a very short time they would lose much of their base of support among organised workers – after all, they were siding with imperialism, with the US government which was relentlessly attacking Perón, and with the old landowning and industrial class against the man who claimed to be speaking for all Argentines, and in particular the poorest.

Ernesto began his high school education in Córdoba, and developed his interest in sport, sex and risk-taking in a defiant response to the weaknesses of his own body. He and his closest friend, Alberto Granado, shared an interest in science, exchanged quotes from great philosophers, and agreed that a career in engineering would be a good thing. In 1948 Che's parents moved to Buenos Aires, though by that time their marriage was entirely on the rocks. Ernesto stayed in Córdoba, though he rushed to the capital when he heard that his grandmother, whom he loved dearly, was close to death. Most of his biographers agree that Che's decision to become a doctor was a personal response to the grief he felt at her passing. Less well known, but probably equally telling in his decision, was his mother's mastectomy following the discovery of breast cancer. Ernesto adored his mother, Celia, always the major presence in his household and his family life.

Che was 19 years old and eligible for military service, though his asthma enabled him to avoid it. He was also now a medical student, though the records of the time suggest a young man more devoted to sexual adventure, whose eclectic reading across philosophy, politics, history, psychoanalysis and Latin American literature suggested a more general restlessness. So his first serious love affair did not make it any less likely that he would relinquish his desire to take off on his motorbike across Argentina and later into Latin America. These were turbulent years in Argentina's political life. And yet, while the young Guevara was clearly opinionated and quite ready to deliver passionate speeches on issues about which he felt strongly, there are few signs of a developing political sense. According to his sister, Ana María:

> He did not take sides one way or the other in relation to
> Perón. He sort of stayed on the sidelines… At least with
> me he never talked politics.[10]

His personal contacts, through his family as well as his friends and companions at university, brought him closer to the bitterly anti-Perónist Radical and Communist parties. Apart from his occasional sexual dalliances with women workers, there is little evidence to suggest that Ernesto had very much contact with working people, from whom he might have gained a rather different sense of how Peronism might be interpreted by other sectors of society.

So, as Che Guevara prepared for his early trips, the image of a restless young adventurer more concerned with the unexpected and the risky seems the most accurate. After his death, as his image grew in significance and depth, biographers and memoirists rushed to find in the life of the young middle-class Argentine some hitherto unrecognised seeds of revolutionary understanding. For the most part those hints and signs are invented. There are certainly suggestions of a human being who felt personal tragedy very deeply, who loved and was loved, who rejoiced in life and was filled with the energy and the reckless confidence of youth. When, two years into his medical degree, he and Alberto visited a leper colony, Che's response was humane and concerned.

But the young Che was no Marxist, and no revolutionary. The realities of an unjust society had not yet impinged on his consciousness in a direct or immediate way. That would come later. The idea that change is possible, that a different world can arise out of the conscious activity of groups in society, had not yet presented itself to him in a convincing way. Events would change that, but as his political awareness grew his interpretations and responses would be influenced, whether he knew it or not, by his early experiences.

Peronism had mobilised masses of working-class people, but in support of an authoritarian figure whose devotion to the people's cause seemed shallow and temporary. In any case, the people with whom the young Ernesto talked politics were unlikely to offer any kind of defence of Perón – they shared his distrust. On the other hand, those around him who claimed to be the guardians of an authentic revolutionary tradition – the Communists and socialists – were a poor lot in the Argentina in which he was growing up. They were rigid, corrupt and manipulative, and unprincipled in their willingness to form alliances with people who should logically have been the enemies of the class they claimed to represent.

When Che came to explore his relationship with the revolutionary tradition, much later, his interpretation of it crucially left out the working class as the agent for social transformation.

3 | Travelling the highways, searching the horizon

> In January and February 1950, during the long summer holiday, having outgrown the great tribal migration to Mar del Plata, Ernesto embarks on a solitary journey which would demand greater stamina, courage and determination than he had ever imagined; a huge circular journey of more than 4,000 kilometres across twelve provinces of northern Argentina. It would leave its mark on him.[11]

Che's father had always been fascinated by the tropical outlands of Paraguay, where the family had lived briefly when Ernesto was young. But there was also another, vast Argentina, both to the north and to the south, which most city dwellers could barely imagine. Che elected to travel north. This was not the urbanised, European, white Argentina that Ernesto had known until then, but a poor, isolated mountain region whose population are closer to the indigenous traditions and history of the High Andes than to the Europe from which so many of Buenos Aires's population came. This region, and especially the province of Salta, would figure large in Che's later life.

In many ways, the history of modern Argentina is a struggle between the city on the banks of the River Plate, whose connections were always with Europe, and an interior – a vast expanse of varied landscapes – whose natural links are with Latin America. The resolution of that struggle late in the 19th century ensured that the country's future would be tied to its external trade, centred on a Buenos Aires that saw itself more and more as a European outpost rather than a Latin American capital.

So Ernesto set out that January of 1950 in the spirit of what Taibo calls '*raidismo*' – that mythical search for an endless Route 66 that leads beyond the horizon. His steed was a rickety motorbike he had largely built himself.[12] For six weeks he travelled, pausing at the leper colony with his friend Alberto, but moving on and ever northwards towards that other indigenous, mountainous, raw and demanding Latin America. There was an excitement in this journey:

> I realised that something that has been growing inside of me for a long time…has matured: it is the hate of civilisation, the absurd image of people moving crazily to the rhythm of the tremendous noise that seems to me like the hateful antithesis of peace.[13]

This is not the declaration of a revolutionary, but of a restless young man desperate to know the world. Ernesto Guevara was driven by what a great 19th century Argentine poet had described as a 'yearning for horizons'. His romantic vision of an unsullied nature would very soon yield, however, to the recognition of the harsh realities of peasant life in these beautiful but unforgiving landscapes.

He returned to medical school in Buenos Aires after

these six long weeks. He passed his exams with no great distinction and devoted himself to a series of moneymaking projects, including the creation of a patent new insecticide. The spray proved to be unbreathable, and none of his other schemes came to very much. In October he fell in love seriously but, as his girlfriend Chichina Ferreyra quickly recognised, nothing at all could contain Che's search for adventure.[14] He was already planning his next, more ambitious trip with Alberto.

It began in October 1951, when the friends climbed aboard the 500cc bike christened La Poderosa – 'The Powerhouse' – and set out for Chile. *The Motorcycle Diaries* describe their two-month trip to the Chilean capital – and the continuing journey without the bike, which gave up on them in Santiago, through the north of Chile, to Peru and eventually to Venezuela.

One biographer describes this journey as 'Che's discovery of America'.[15] The diaries, while they are still the chronicles of a young man on the open road – laughing, flirting, taking risks, conning and charming his way from town to town – are also the record of a developing consciousness. From Buenos Aires and Córdoba to this was more than a physical distance. It was also an encounter with Latin America, with an alternative past, with the long resistance of people who recognisably belonged to that other history.

There were certain key encounters on that journey. In northern Chile, for example, Che and Alberto came face to face with the huge copper mines, gouged out of the extraordinary and timelessly beautiful desert landscape, dusty and brutal, their great machines like mechanical mouths gulping lumps out of the sand. This was Chile's major source of wealth and foreign currency – yet when Che saw it all this wealth belonged to foreign multinationals, like Kennecott and Anaconda, who bought and sold the copper on the foreign markets and exchanges which they dominated.

Che's diary entries for these days are fairly noncommittal, though he recognises that the mines are tombs to thousands of miners. The old Communist miner he met there evoked his respect and admiration, but it is still a little fanciful to suggest that the visit was a kind of road to Damascus moment for Che, when suddenly everything became clear to him.[16] Che's comments are interesting and thoughtful, but they are also the words of an observer, of someone in transit and registering this world for the first time – curious, but still relatively unengaged.

Peru, on the other hand, does seem to have had a powerful emotional impact. As they crossed the border from Bolivia into Peru, Che comments with perplexity on the indigenous people he sees along the roadside – oppressed, afraid and excluded. But it is when he reaches the wonderful mountain city of Machu Picchu, 17,000 feet above sea level in the High Andes above Cuzco, that he seems overcome by it all. The site of a late Inca resistance to Spanish conquest, Machu Picchu was abandoned after the defeat of the Incas and forgotten until it was excavated by a Harvard archaeologist early in the 20th century. Its tall temples and stepped terraces mimic the mountain – its walls, as the Spaniards found when they tried to destroy them, were built to last forever.

There is a snapshot of Che standing under the square-arched door of one of the temples. The architecture and the power of this place took his breath away. At that moment the reality of the great pre-Columbian empires must have come home to him – the sense of that other America, so long invisible, silenced and oppressed. In some passages of his diaries there are references to the destructive role of foreign empires, Spanish and North

American, and to the power of Indo-America. After all, he was an Argentine from the city, whose knowledge of that world was as limited as any European.

Their travels continued into the Amazon, where he and Alberto spent a little time at a leper colony and Che wrestled with his asthma in the conditions of jungle living, before moving on to Venezuela, Miami and home. The trip taught him a great deal. It had shown him what it meant to be a Latin American, and it had made him restless, curious, anxious for understanding. His attitude to what he saw in the leper colony suggests a man of humane and generous spirit. Perhaps these are the preconditions for a person to become a revolutionary. But they are not enough on their own. Revolutionaries must have that profound sense of injustice, of course, but they also need the driving vision of a different world, a clear sense of whose class interests and values will shape it, and of how that class can organise to overthrow the old order and usher in the new.

Che wanted to leave again as soon as he arrived back in Argentina, but he bowed to family pressure and agreed to take his final medical exams.

He worked day and night at the National Library in Buenos Aires, preparing for the 15 papers he still needed to pass. In April 1953, a little over six months after his return from Miami, Che phoned his parents to tell them that he was now a doctor – and to announce, at the same time, that he was preparing his next Latin American journey. His mother Celia lamented, 'I'll never see him again – I know I won't.' She did see her son again, a few years later, but by then things had changed dramatically.

7 July 1953 was a grey, wet day in Buenos Aires's Retiro railway station. Che and his childhood friend Carlos Calica Ferrer found a seat, then waved goodbye to

Celia. As they pulled away from the platform, Che shouted, 'I'm going to be a soldier for Latin America.' It was accidentally prophetic – but at this stage the only plan Che had was to meet up again with Alberto and return to the leper colony in the Amazon.

Three thousand kilometres later the travellers arrived in Bolivia's capital, La Paz. It was an extraordinary time in Bolivia. Just over a year earlier a revolution led by the workers' federation of Bolivia (COB), and the miners' union in particular, had put in place a new nationalist government. When Che arrived the debate about how far and in what direction the revolution could go was still raging. At the heart of it was an argument about seizing the country's wealth – particularly its mines – and using their profits to begin to raise the living standards of the poor and terribly exploited Aymara-speaking miners of the High Andes. The tragic irony, of course, was that the two or three wealthy individuals who owned Bolivia's valuable deposits of tin had made billions – and invested their huge profits in Europe and North America. Bolivia's richest tin baron, Simon Patiño, for instance, owned P&O shipping lines and lived in a suite in New York's Waldorf Astoria, not to mention his mansions in Paris, Madrid and elsewhere. When the revolution came, finally, the mines were almost exhausted – but Patiño never returned the money he had made from 50 years of brutal exploitation of Bolivian workers.[17]

Imagine the conditions of life in mines at 10,000 feet and above in the beautiful but harsh Andean range. The wind is always bitterly cold, the dust is constant, and the miners live in the most extreme poverty in villages clinging to the mountainside. What little they have they have fought for – in long, brutal strikes which have always brought death and repression in their wake.

The 1952 revolution was in some ways the revenge of

history – or it should have been. Instead the leaders of the workers' movement entered into a series of alliances with nationalist politicians who led the process away from the demands and interests of Bolivia's workers. When, 15 years later, Che returned to Bolivia in very different circumstances, the miners were still fighting.

In 1953, however, while he was aware of the tensions in the country, Che still described himself (in a letter to his father) as a 'neutral spectator'. He was a keen observer, excited by what was going on around him, but as likely to write at length about his amorous adventures or the intricate technicalities of mine engineering as about politics. In a letter to Tita Infante, a friend in Argentina, he did describe the political situation – the unstable balance of forces amid rumours of an imminent counter-revolution.[18] And he was angered by the patronising and racist treatment of the indigenous people waiting at the Ministry of Peasant Affairs.

He watched, he was interested and curious, but still distant. In the recently published diary of his second trip, Che spends very little time discussing what was without doubt one of the most *politically* important moments of his trip (a recent revolution at a crossroads). Instead he seems anxious to move on and return to the magnificent Inca sites of Peru which he had visited earlier.

High on the Andean plateau, Ernesto and Carlos sailed Lake Titicaca and crossed the Bolivian-Peruvian border at the cold and barren town of Puno. The customs confiscated a couple of books (a Bolivian government publication and a copy of *Man in the Soviet Union*) before letting them travel on to Cuzco, the Inca capital that had so fascinated Guevara on his first journey. From there they journeyed on to Lima, the capital of Peru, where Che met up again with Hugo Pesce, the Communist doctor who, according to the dedication he wrote for him in his copy of *Guerrilla Warfare*, 'provoked a great change in my attitude towards life and society'.

The journey continued and the travellers decided to make for Guatemala, in Central America. That visit would prove to be the turning point in Che's life. Guatemala, too, was in the midst of a process of social upheaval and change. Later biographers and commentators have suggested that this is why Che decided to go there – that he was in search of revolution. But there is no evidence to support that idea. It was, at that stage, just another phase in the journey. But there is no doubt that *after* Guatemala travelling would take on a very different meaning and a very different purpose.

4 | **The banana republic**

> Before Guatemala the Argentine's journey had been important, but only in an emotional and cultural sense. Now Ernesto Che Guevara would experience his true political rite of passage... Doubtless Guevara had arrived with an already heavy ideological load in his worn knapsack, but he would leave Guatemala with entire trunks full of ideas, affinities, hatreds and judgements.[19]

Another biographer puts it slightly differently:

> By the time he arrived in Guatemala, Ernesto seems to have undergone a political conversion – or at least he was trying to talk himself into one.[20]

In a sense, it is all speculation based on what would happen later. What is beyond question is that Guevara left Guatemala eight months after his arrival a different person.

Of course, he had some political insights and attitudes before he arrived in Guatemala City in December 1953.

Anderson sets great store by a note Che added to his travel diaries as an afterthought.[21] It describes a conversation with an unnamed old revolutionary which uncannily predicts Guevara's own death, although in very general terms. It is a rhetorical, rather melodramatic piece shot through with visions of revolutionary heroism and the language of sacrifice and death. It is not really a political document at all, but it does suggest an idea of the heroic and the dramatic that seems to course through all the writing and thought of Che Guevara.

In Peru he had come face to face, in the great Inca fortress of Machu Picchu, with the grandeur of Indian America and the absolute destruction wreaked by the Spanish conquerors, the first imperialists. In Bolivia he had encountered racism and the spirit of resistance in the faces of the miners. He expressed his deep distaste for the opportunistic politicians who manipulated the masses – people like Juan Lechín, leader of the Bolivian trades union congress. They reminded him too much, perhaps, of the slippery and manipulative Juan Perón.

Yet before his arrival in Guatemala there is no sense in his writings or in other people's memories of him that Che felt any kind of personal commitment to the cause of liberation, or saw any place for himself in political struggle. This is not to cast doubt on his later revolutionary commitment, only to recognise that revolutionaries are not born, they are not above ordinary life. People *become* revolutionaries as they see how the world is, understand the pressing need for change and come to identify the forces that can make this happen.

Guatemala in 1953 was still an Indian country – 60 percent of its population were indigenous descendants of the Maya civilisation which dominated southern Mexico and Central America for centuries before the arrival of the

Spanish. Guatemalan Maya resistance to conquest was not fully over until the mid-17th century, and there was a continuing history of defensive struggles by the Maya communities against the assaults and depredations of the colonial landowners, a tiny white elite who continued to control the nation's land and wealth after the departure of the Spanish.

A coffee economy through most of the 19th century, the growing US market for bananas and coffee, both of which grew liberally in Guatemala's fertile soil, brought marauding US companies to the country. For the first 40 years of the 20th century the history of Guatemala is the history of one major North American company, United Fruit, and its founder and owner, Sam Zemurray.[22]

A succession of military dictatorships had kept Guatemala tied to the powerful external demands of the United Fruit Company. By the early 1940s, under the guiding hand of General Jorge Ubico, some 40 percent of Guatemala's land was under the control of the company known throughout Central America as La Yunai. Then, in 1944, a new government under Rafael Arévalo announced a programme of reform. After all, President Franklin Roosevelt had announced the United States's commitment to the 'four democratic freedoms' towards the end of the Second World War. The enormous gap between rich and poor in Guatemala, and the control of its economy by a single foreign company, surely made it an ideal candidate for democratic change.

The key to Arévalo's programme, logically enough, was land reform – the redistribution of United Fruit's properties among the landless communities – together with social programmes that included trade union rights and a programme of popular education. Elections in 1951 brought to government a young military officer who had served under Arévalo – Jacobo Arbenz – to carry the programme through to its completion. In 1952 he signed a land reform decree which nationalised the lands of United Fruit and other major landowners.

It is important to emphasise that Arbenz was no revolutionary. In a sense, his project was the modernisation of the economy under a Guatemalan state able to control and determine the allocation of its own resources. But the process of fairly moderate reform that he set in motion unleashed other forces which he could not easily control. The organisations of workers, particularly of agricultural workers and peasants, seized the opportunity to make sure that the promised changes would happen. The process, therefore, was announced from above but driven from below.

In the United States, of course, the situation was viewed with alarm and rage. This was the era of the Cold War, the consequence of the division of the world between two zones of power – the Soviet bloc, with the Soviet Union at its heart, and the United States, the larger and more powerful of the two. They were separated by what Churchill had called the 'Iron Curtain' – a dividing line at once military, political and ideological. In this atmosphere, all attempts at social change were immediately characterised as incipient Communism – the creeping influence of the Soviets. And this in turn could justify direct military intervention by the United States – as it already had in a number of places across the world.

Thus the Guatemalan reforms were described in Washington as a threat of Communism in the backyard. As it happened, several key figures in the Washington government were intimately involved with the United Fruit Company – among them John Foster Dulles, Secretary of State, and his brother Allen Dulles, head of the CIA. They shared their hatred of the Guatemalan government both with the wealthy landowners of Guatemala itself and with the dictatorial rulers of the nearby Central American countries of El Salvador, Honduras and Nicaragua. Together they organised the overthrow of Arbenz, which was to be led by a US-financed military force under Carlos Castillo Armas.[23]

Che arrived in Guatemala City, the country's capital, just six months before the overthrow of Arbenz. The real confrontations and conflicts were developing in the countryside, but the atmosphere in the capital was still agitated and politicised, particularly since the Latin American left was so well represented there. Socialists and revolutionaries had arrived in Guatemala from all over the continent – some because they had been driven into exile, others because they were curious to see at first hand how the process would develop.

Che's own reasons for being there were mixed, but there is no doubt that he was becoming increasingly politically aware. An anti-imperialism he had already expressed in very general terms now became concrete as he watched the preparations the United States was making to bring down Arbenz. Washington was clearly working hand in hand with the United Fruit Company. It was equally clear that any reforms or improvements that affected US interests would immediately be denounced as Soviet intervention. Writing to his Aunt Beatriz from Guatemala, Che announced, 'I have adopted a firm position alongside the Guatemalan government and within it the Communist PGT'.[24] In other ways, too, he expressed a romantic attachment to things Russian – a residue no doubt of his connections with Argentine Communists through his mother.

At a fairly basic level, the intransigence of the North Americans encouraged Che's instinctive feeling that there was no alternative to armed resistance. When the coup did come, and Guatemala City was bombarded from the air for a week, there was very little armed resistance. The reasons why are still a matter of debate. The most plausible explanation, however, seems to be that when Arbenz refused to consider arming the workers, hopes of successful resistance faded rapidly. He resigned within a week of the first air attacks, which were combined with an invasion by groups of soldiers from neighbouring Honduras.

The coup was not unexpected. On 2 February Che had written to his father to say that an invasion was imminent. By the end of the month several of the exiles had left in anticipation of the attack. In March an InterAmerican Conference controlled by Washington's friends passed a motion threatening any states which might represent a 'hemispheric threat' – a clear and direct reference to Guatemala. The forces were gathering, and it was obvious to everyone. Yet Che chose this moment to take a short trip to look at archaeological sites in El Salvador and Honduras. By the time he returned to Guatemala at the end of May, the tension was palpable. Everyone knew that invasion was imminent.

The 'official' historians of Che's life, particularly those in Cuba, have claimed that he was involved, both politically and militarily, in preparing the resistance. There is no evidence to support this. His trip in May suggests he did not feel particularly integrated, and just a few weeks previously he had expressed a desire to leave the country because he was having difficulty finding work. It was a combination of lack of money and what seemed like a job offer that moved him to change his plans.

At the same time he was clearly concerned about and keenly aware of what was happening in those weeks. At a more abstract level his political education was progressing in new directions. The Latin Americans whom he had met and socialised with since his arrival were almost all politically involved. And he was also increasingly attached to a Peruvian political activist, Hilda Gadea, who was becoming in some ways his political mentor. Their personal relationship was less clear. She helped and supported him, introduced him to new friends and connections, and patiently explored a range of revolutionary ideas with him. She was not typical of the beautiful young women Che normally pursued – and perhaps it is right, in the end, to acknowledge that this was more a profound political friendship than an expression of sexual desire. Nonetheless, until his arrival in Cuba, Hilda would be a formative political influence on him:

> Che's stay in the Mayan nation was not a period of passionate sentiments, but of political awakening.[25]

These elements – a deep anti-imperialism, a developing awareness of Marxist and socialist ideas, a residual devotion to an idealised Soviet Union, a deep impatience with corruption – were being defined in Guatemala. They did not, however, lead him to take any defined role in the days of the coup – he had registered to be a doctor working with the fighters, but he never had the opportunity to join the battle in any capacity.

His diaries at the time express his frustration with and to some extent his incomprehension of how events are unfolding. On 20 June 1954 he assures his mother, 'The people's spirits are very high. There is a real climate of struggle.' Writing three days later, after the sudden resignation of President Arbenz, he tells her that 'a terrible cold shower has fallen on all those who admire Guatemala'. He is clear that it is Washington and its allies who are responsible for what is to come.

Reflecting on the speed of events, he writes to Celia again on 4 July:

> It has all been a beautiful dream from which you are in no hurry to awake… Once more the aphorism is confirmed that sees the liquidation of the army as the true principle of democracy… The harsh truth is that Arbenz did not know how to rise to the occasion.[26]

Che noticed, too, that the political leadership of the movement from below, and the Guatemalan Communist Party (the PGT) in particular, failed to provide leadership when the moment came – because they too accepted the obligation to follow Arbenz.

Yet Che did not explore these issues in any great depth. The lack of weapons and military organisation, as far as he was concerned, were key:

> He could have given arms to the people, but he did not want to… Now we see the result.[27]

On the face of it, that was the key issue – and one to which Che would return in his conversations and arguments with friends. Hilda reports that Che was growing more and more agitated as he watched the process unfold from his temporary hospital post – and could do nothing. It was frustrating and difficult. When the new military government under Castillo Armas took power, the repression grew more severe. There were about 700 Latin Americans in Guatemala who had come to be part of what they imagined would be an increasingly radical political experiment. Now many of them hurriedly left, while others took refuge in the various embassies.

Hilda's political background made her particularly

vulnerable, but she could not leave without a visa. Che eventually decided to seek asylum in the Argentine embassy. His diary describes days of boredom and worsening asthma. To while away the time he crafted small pen portraits of his fellow exiles. He wrote several of them off for their lack of political education, although Ricardo Ramírez, who would later become a key figure in the Guatemalan armed resistance, impressed him greatly.[28]

It is clear that Che now considered himself to be a communist – he is scathing, for example, about one of his fellow embassy refugees, whom he calls:

> A man of average intelligence, he is sufficiently capable
> to realise that the only ideal road for the working class is
> communism.[29]

Nevertheless, there is very little in his writings of the time to suggest that he is yet addressing the questions of organisation, education and consciousness that flow from thinking of yourself as a communist. The one issue he returns to over and over again when he reviews the coup and its aftermath is the question of arms. Yet had the Guatemalan people been given arms without the political organisation to determine when and how they should be used, the results could easily have been as disastrous as they were after the overthrow of Arbenz. And the reason they were not distributed is not because of the personal weakness of Arbenz himself, but because the parties in a position to lead that struggle were themselves unprepared and vacillating.

At this stage of his life, Che does not give the impression that these matters were at the forefront of his mind. The one thing that was certain was that he would leave Guatemala – it was no longer safe for any foreign sympathiser of Arbenz to remain. Yet he was determined he would not return to Argentina but move on to Mexico for what he described as 'the next stage of my adventure'.

His journey thus far had been a preparation for the moment when Ernesto Guevara would be transformed into El Che. The next phase would mark out a new and very different road for him.

5 | **The Cuban dimension**

Many of the Latin American exiles had already gone to Mexico. During the Spanish Civil War the Mexican government had welcomed Spanish Republican refugees. Although it was dominated by a corrupt and authoritarian (though elected) presidency, Mexico carefully preserved its reputation as a haven for political exiles – and not only from Guatemala. Among those who had found refuge in Mexico there were also a number of Cubans.

This was late September 1954, and Che was travelling towards Mexico City. He had only one contact there – an ageing poet who worked in the film industry. But the closest Che got to the cinema was an encounter with a Spanish refugee who lent him a camera so he could take pictures of families and strolling lovers in Chapultepec Park in the city. To this he added a part-time job in an allergy clinic and a chance encounter that produced a job sorting photographs in a press agency.

Che was surviving. When Hilda arrived he still had no fixed place to live, and they met several times a week in

hotels and cafes. Che seemed anxious to marry the pregnant Hilda, which they would do later, but she was more
wary. She probably realised that this handsome young man
who enjoyed brief encounters would be a difficult partner.
But politically she was still his reference point, although in
Mexico City Che was making or renewing political friend-
ships. One old Cuban friend, Ñico López, spoke to him at
some length about the armed opposition in Cuba. They
were fateful conversations.

Che moved in political circles now, and his letters home
often expressed his rage against the imperialist power to
the north, a rage born of what he had seen in Guatemala.
Yet he was still essentially a wanderer, a man with multiple
travel plans and a deep resistance to any kind of collective
discipline. In a letter to his mother, he wrote:

> The [Guatemalan] Communists are worthy of respect
> and sooner or later I will join the party; more than any-
> thing else what impedes me from doing it now is that I
> still have a fantastic urge to travel through Europe and I
> couldn't do that submitted to an iron discipline.[30]

By November 1954, from his own point of view at
least, Che had crossed an important line. He was not yet
the full-time revolutionary he became, and he had no
clear sense of what it meant in practice to become one.
He rarely discussed strategy and tactics. Yet his sense of
personal commitment was already intense, and he had
begun to develop a vision of how his own life might now
unfold.

In the early months of 1955 Che held several jobs, and
was spending more and more time with the group of
Cuban exiles. Some writers suggest that they seemed less
prone to dreams and nostalgic conversations than some of

the other Latin American exiles. That is a harsh judgement to make about people, many of whom went on to fight and die in the cause of justice in Latin America. But it was certainly the case that the Cubans seemed well organised and engaged in a very immediate way in a rapidly changing situation at home. And although Che's eyes were still fixed on Europe, the Cubans had now convinced him that Cuba should figure in his future plans.

On 26 July 1953 a group of armed men had attempted to storm the Moncada barracks in Cuba. The assault was a failure, and a number of those involved were killed. The others, including the leader of the group, Fidel Castro, were arrested. One year earlier, the man who had dominated Cuban politics since the 1930s – Fulgencio Batista – had seized power and annulled imminent elections. For Castro it was the definitive sign that democratic change was impossible in Cuba. Batista was supported by the United States, which regarded him as an important component of the chain of anti-Communist regimes it had established or encouraged across Latin America. What President Roosevelt had said about Somoza, the ruler of Nicaragua, applied equally to Batista: 'He's a son of a bitch, but he's our son of a bitch.'

Cuba had been the last Spanish colony in the Americas. It achieved its independence only in 1898 after a three-year war. But real independence was short-lived. This war continues to be referred to in the US as the Spanish-American War. The presence of US troops on the island, and their involvement in expelling the Spanish army, shaped Cuban independence in a way never envisaged in the writings of José Martí, the political leader of Cuba's struggle against colonialism who was killed in 1895 at the beginning of the second and decisive liberation war.

Using a device that would later become familiar in US

dealings with the rest of the world, Washington intervened directly in Cuban affairs with the justification it was defending the 'interests of US citizens'. A mysterious explosion aboard the USS *Maine* while it was in Havana harbour provided the pretext for the 1901 Platt Amendment – a clause inserted in the *Cuban* constitution which permitted the US to act on Cuban soil whenever it deemed its interests to be threatened. In addition, Guantánamo Bay was ceded on a 99-year lease as a base for the US Navy. Washington nominated the head of the national bank, the customs service and the police. It was an early step in the incorporation of Cuba into the US economy – as a supplier of the sugar that was becoming so important a component of the new urban diet, and as a market for US goods.

> Cuba passed smoothly from a state of colonisation to one of neo-colonisation. Within the first three years of independence, over 13,000 land speculators and investors arrived from the US and bought up an estimated 60 percent of the land.[31]

US capital consolidated its domination over the economy. Sugar prices were sky-high in the three years to 1920. More and more land was given to sugar cultivation, and more and more investment directed to the industry. Then prices collapsed and many of the larger local producers went bankrupt. Their lands were sold to US firms, so that by 1921 these owned the bulk of Cuba's large sugar plantations and imported most of its sugar.[32]

The crash of the US economy in 1929 and the Depression that followed hit Cuba hard. As living standards fell and unemployment rose with the decline in sugar exports, popular resentment against the corrupt and toadying Machado regime then in power grew. In 1933 that resentment exploded in a series of protests, strikes and demonstrations which brought Machado down. In the heat of these months of resistance and struggle, workers' soviets were briefly set up under Communist leadership. Students, led by the members of the Directorio Revolucionario, the Revolutionary Directorate, took a key role – so much so that the leader of the noncommissioned officers in the army, the mulatto son of a cane-cutter, Fulgencio Batista, called upon the students to name the new president of the country. Their choice, a university professor called Grau San Martín, introduced the eight-hour day, rescinded the Platt Amendment and announced the coming nationalisation of the electricity industry.

But the new republic lasted no more than a few months, as Batista certainly anticipated. The new government was, in turn, overthrown by a revolt of the noncommissioned officers in the army – the so-called sergeants' revolt led by Batista – which had the tacit support of the US government.

It was 1940 before Batista himself came to the presidency, although he had ruled since 1934 from behind the presidential throne. When he did take power, it was with the support of Cuba's Communist Party, the PSP. This seemed a strange marriage, particularly since the Communist Party's influence had grown during the period of social upheavals and protests in 1933 which was brought to a premature end by the sergeants' revolt. That revolt expressed a demand for an end to US control of Cuba's economy and state, but it stopped well short of the pressure for social revolution that the practice of the 1933 revolts had placed on the agenda. It was a greater degree of national independence that the sergeants demanded in their more radical moments, not the establishment of workers' power.

By 1940, however, the situation had changed in important ways. The Communist parties across the world adopted a policy of collaboration with liberals, radicals, even conservative groupings, in the so-called popular fronts. This strategy was not a consequence of the particular conditions operating in any one country, but the result of the Soviet Union's concern to build a wide international coalition against Nazism and break out of its isolation in the face of German expansion. That meant finding common ground with a whole range of social forces that were bitterly hostile to the ideals of socialism and communism – but who might agree on a broad anti-fascist platform. Stalin, the leader of the Soviet Union, and his Communist allies across the world were quite ready to pay the price of this broad front if it would lessen Russia's isolation and vulnerability. But its political cost was enormous and the repercussions broad and lasting, for it involved to all intents and purposes abandoning the struggle to replace capitalism with a more authentically democratic socialist system. In Spain, for example, the consequence was that the Communist Party opposed the development of a revolutionary response to the fascist uprising of 1936 and instead threw in its lot with a coalition of centre and right wing parties whose one unifying feature was their fear of a workers' revolution.[33]

The strange liaison of Batista and the PSP was the product of that wider political imperative. The Cuban Communists were heavily influenced (for fairly obvious reasons) by the Communist Party of the US, whose leader, Earl Browder, was an enthusiast for the popular front policy.[34] In the late 1930s the United States, under the presidency of Franklin Roosevelt, was recovering from the Depression era through a series of state-sponsored projects, such as the construction of the Tennessee Valley Dam. Roosevelt's New Deal spoke a language of social inclusion and nation-building (or rebuilding). It seemed almost a manifestation of the popular front, and Browder, in his anxiety to create a coalition, volunteered to dissolve the Communist Party. This policy of extreme collaboration became known as Browderism. The Cuban Communists, it seemed, were equally keen to make gestures of conciliation and to seek alliances with forces to their right.

Their reward was the inclusion of two Communist ministers in Batista's cabinet – Juan Marinello, the party leader, and Carlos Rafael Rodríguez, a 30 year old Communist who would play a key role in Cuban politics half a century later. In one sense their inclusion in government brought the party a share of power. Communists were central to the growth of militant trade unions through the 1930s – now they threw that influence behind the coalition government. There were some benefits: the labour ministry agreed a number of concessions to the stronger unions in exchange for their support. But the Communists in government fulfilled a very different role from those who had led working-class struggles just a few years earlier. From their position in the state, they became the instrument for reconciling the interests of the state and those of the workers, and this could only hold back the capacity of the workers' organisations to act *independently* of the state.

Batista was followed into the presidential palace by Grau San Martín (in 1944) and then by the slippery and corrupt Prío Socarrás (in 1948). The Communists also supported the Grau government. Yet in 1947 their erstwhile ally turned against them. After all, the war was over and in the post-war world the US and the Soviets were rival empires locked in a Cold War. The wartime alliance gave way to a new climate of conflict and confrontation – and the short-lived coalitions of Latin America were among the early casualties in this new kind of warfare.

In 1945 Fidel Castro Ruz entered the law faculty of the

University of Havana. He was 19 years old, the son of a fairly wealthy landowning family of Spanish extraction from the east of the island. Like many middle-class student nationalists, he was suspicious of the Communists inside the university and outside it. In Cuba, as elsewhere, they had colluded with governments that were corrupt and authoritarian in exchange for support for the Soviet Union. Communism was a discredited and corrupted notion by the time Castro's generation encountered it. Yet he and his contemporaries were bitterly hostile to the Batista regime and to the imperialist interests that still controlled Cuba's economy.

If Communism no longer represented the politics of anti-imperialist resistance, the alternative was the kind of radical nationalism represented by the Directorio Revolucionario (the Student Revolutionary Directorate) which in some ways preserved and symbolised the revolutionary aspirations of 1933. It advocated direct action and armed confrontation with the state. As a consequence it worked largely in secret.

In 1948 Castro was involved in a curious adventure which proved to be a pointer to his future activity. With a small group of fellow students he organised military training on an isolated quay in the Caribbean. Its purpose was to prepare an armed invasion of the Dominican Republic, then already oppressed by the 30-year dictatorship of the cruel dictator Trujillo.[35] The invasion never happened – the project turned into a series of mishaps and misunderstandings, and came to nothing.

Back in Havana, Fidel became involved with the Ortodoxo party led by Eduardo Chibas, a famous radio personality, and was a candidate for Congress for the 1952 elections. Late in 1951 Chibas killed himself on air in a gesture of protest that almost certainly went wrong. Soon afterwards, Batista launched his coup and cut short the electoral process, as many people expected. His immediate actions once in power were a sign of things to come: he banned political parties, filled the state with his cronies and launched a campaign of repression. For Castro, this served only to confirm what he had almost certainly always believed – that the democratic process could not bring change, and the actions of small, determined groups alone could take power from dictatorial regimes.

The Moncada attack was the first act of a new strategy. Brought to trial for the assault, Castro was unapologetic. His long speech from the dock (though relatively short by his later standards) announced that 'history would absolve him'. It served as a kind of manifesto for the group he would form two years later, when he was released under a government amnesty. To commemorate the Moncada attack the organisation was called the 26 July Movement (M-26-J). Its declared objective was the armed overthrow of the Batista regime and the construction of an independent national state:

> We were taught that you do not beg for liberty; it is won with machete in hand. José Martí said, 'The man who abides by unjust laws and permits anyone to trample the country in which he was born is not an honourable man.'
>
> I do not fear prison, any more than I fear the fury of the miserable tyrant who took the lives of 70 of my comrades at Moncada.
>
> Condemn me. It doesn't matter. History will absolve me.[36]

With these words from the dock Castro placed himself at the centre of Cuban political life – and turned what had been a defeat into a kind of moral victory. The rest of his long speech was the statement of a radical nationalist. It insisted on the demand for genuine economic and political independence from external influence, and condemned Batista in the harshest terms. Yet, paradoxically, it was in many ways a restatement of the unfulfilled aims and purposes of the revolt that Batista had led in 1934.

The Cuban Communists were unimpressed. Castro was a student leader married to an idea of armed confrontation with the state, he was contemptuous of the Communist tradition and certainly had no experience of or connection with working-class struggles. They distrusted him, and he in turn was bitterly hostile to a party which he saw as totally compromised and sullied by its long involvement with the dictator. As a result, Castro remained distanced from ideas of socialism or suspicious of any idea that workers might be central to any process of social transformation.

The Directorio still existed. In 1957 its members attempted to kill Batista in the National Palace. Instead, all the members of the group were killed, including their charismatic leader José Antonio Echavarria, leaving Castro with no rivals for the leadership of the armed movement.

Two years after his arrest, Castro was released from prison under a government amnesty. The irony is that while Fidel and his brother Raúl were released along with other members of the group, there was no amnesty for imprisoned Communists. Perhaps the US advisers behind Batista did not recognise Castro as a threat. In any event, Castro remained in Cuba for a few weeks while Raúl went to Mexico to prepare for his brother's arrival.

At university Raúl had read the Marxist classics and grown close to the Communists. He was, from then on, the link between the Communist Party and the leadership of the 26 July Movement, the bridge between the two mutually suspicious groups. He fled Cuba after he was denounced by the Batista government as the person responsible for a series of explosions in Havana. In Mexico Che Guevara was one of a group waiting to welcome him:

> Raúl spoke of his faith in his older brother and of his personal belief, echoing Ernesto's view, that in Cuba and the rest of the region power could be gained not through elections, but only through war. With popular support one could gain power and then transform society from capitalism to socialism.[37]

This reported conversation is telling. For Raúl, despite his broad background reading in Marxism, clearly did not share that most central of ideas – evolved by Lenin out of Marx – that revolution must of necessity be 'the act of the working class itself'. Socialism involved a wholly different understanding of power. When Marx called himself a revolutionary democrat, he envisaged a wholly new kind of democracy in which the majority in society, the people who produced the wealth, would become its governors.

For Raúl and Fidel, change could be the result of the armed actions of a minority. They, and not the working class, would be the subjects of this process of change. This way of understanding what it meant to be a revolutionary reflected the group's middle-class background – but much more importantly it betrayed the political distance between them and workers. Their project foresaw an independent *state* which could decree change in society from above.

In this process, the main instrument was not mass organisation or the power of workers, but the arms held by the revolutionaries. Political forces were less central than the force of arms.

Che was won over by this argument because it corre-
sponded to the conclusions he had drawn from his experience in Guatemala. It was this shared conviction that drew
him and Raúl together. Two weeks later, around 7 or 8
July, Che met Fidel. He arrived home in a state of excitement. 'Ñico was right,' he told Hilda. 'Fidel Castro will
make the revolution.' Two years later he explained to an
Argentine journalist:

> I thought Fidel was extraordinary. He had an absolute
> faith that once he set out for Cuba he'd get there, and
> that when he got there he would fight, and that he'd win.
> I shared his optimism. You had to act, to struggle, to do
> what you said you were going to do. You had to stop
> weeping and fight.[38]

A few days later, Hilda records, Che had made his decision to join Castro's planned armed landing in Cuba.

Fidel later claimed that Che was much more ideological, clearer in his political convictions, than he was himself.
Others have enthusiastically agreed. The reality, I suspect,
was a little different. Che himself called Karl Marx, rather
whimsically, 'Saint Charlie'. He had certainly begun to read
Marx, though we are not told which of his writings engaged
Che's attention. But he was also writing an article on the
function of doctors in Latin America at the time, as well as
developing some ideas in the field of allergy treatments.

In August Che married Hilda Gadea in Tepozotlán, a
little town not far from Mexico City which was famous for
its pre-Hispanic sites. Raúl Castro was present, although
he could not sign as an official witness – his presence in
Mexico was still a secret. In letters to the family announc-
ing the marriage, Che still writes about the journeys he
intends to undertake – to Europe, to Africa. Hilda was

pregnant with their daughter Beatriz.

Clearly, this is the moment at which El Che emerges out of the life of Ernesto Guevara. It is a strange cross-roads. While Che himself announces confidently that 'Saint Charlie [Marx] is now the axis [of my life]',[39] there is no sense in the many accounts we have of this time in his life that he was devoting himself to political education or that he was thinking his way through the big issues of socialist history. He remained a complex and sometimes contradictory man.

We know that Che was humane and generous in his concerns for the poor and the needy and the suffering. We know he was full of energy and enthusiasm, restless and dynamic, and that this spirit affected and infected the people he met. Most of all, however, you sense a kind of frustration in him, a feeling that the enemy (imperialism) is known and the task is clear, albeit expressed in very general terms – to make a better world, to achieve freedom and justice. Politically, it is clear Che's sympathies were with a Communist tradition of which he was still not particularly knowledgeable. He watched the overthrow of Perón in Argentina in September 1955 with a kind of detachment, although he was deeply concerned at the violence that followed Perón's fall.

It was not Argentina but his experience in Guatemala that seemed definitive for Che. He drew the conclusion that action was the key to everything. As Fidel himself put it later:

> In those days in Mexico we did not discuss revolutionary theory. What we discussed was the struggle against Batista, the plan to disembark in Cuba, initiating guerrilla warfare… It was Che's fighting spirit, as a man of action, that led him to join me in the struggle.[40]

This was what attracted Fidel and Che to one another – a kind of reckless courage, a yearning to act, and a firm belief that the success or failure of a revolution depended exclusively on the determination and training of a small group of committed revolutionaries.

They were both products of their time. The revolutionary socialist tradition associated with the Communist parties had been thoroughly discredited by its association with regimes in Eastern Europe that were tyrannical and oppressive. In Latin America, the readiness of the Communists to compromise with parties and organisations of the right served to empty Marxist ideas of any meaning. It would be several years later[41] before the mask would begin to fall from Stalinism and the Communist parties which spoke in its defence would lose their claim to the ownership of a socialist tradition. In the meantime, a new generation of revolutionaries looked elsewhere for their politics.

6 | **82 men and a boat**

For a time at least, the lives of these two men would be inextricably connected. They had a great deal in common, yet they were very different.

However abstract it might have been, Che's commitment was to social change. Even then, when his political education was still at a relatively early stage, Che was a passionate advocate of a different society. In a way, his ideas on these matters were probably more clearly expressed in his discussion of the role of the doctor – as a servant of the neediest in society – and in his general anti-imperialism. Unlike Fidel, he now occasionally described himself as a communist, even if he was less than clear about what it meant.

Castro was much more obviously an ambitious politician whose gaze was set on power. Fidel was impatient with political debate and deeply suspicious of the socialism that he later came to represent for so many people. He was also convinced of his place in history – his speech from the dock left no doubt about that.

Politically, Fidel and Che were very different too. Fidel was a nationalist with a declared political programme which was limited to five demands centred on land reform, an end to corruption and the re-establishment of the constitution of 1940. Support for these policies came not only from workers and peasants, but also from a number of business people who helped Castro financially. It was this support that enabled him to buy a motor launch, *Granma*, and finance the guerrilla training camps near Chalco in Mexico. Guevara, on the other hand, described himself as a revolutionary and a communist. There was no question of where power lay within the 26 July Movement, of course. Fidel was its uncontested leader.

Many writers have tried to explain or rationalise the relationship between the two men:

> Both were favoured boys from large families and extremely spoiled; careless about their appearance; sexually voracious, but men to whom relationships came in second to their personal goals. Both were imbued with Latin machismo; believers in the innate weakness of women, contemptuous of homosexuals and admirers of brave men of action.[42]

Castro quickly recognised Che's qualities – his passion, his commitment, his restlessness. By the end of 1955 it was clear that Fidel intended to give Che a leading role in the preparations for the Cuban Revolution, but it would be limited to matters of training and practical tasks. Politically Fidel and Che were still a long way apart. Yet Che did not challenge or argue with Fidel. Perhaps it was Fidel's charisma that held Che back. Fidel was certainly a forceful, dominant personality. Che deferred to him. He admired this man of unshakeable resolution and conviction in his own destiny. And after

all, Che was involved in a foreign invasion. He knew little about Cuba and accepted Fidel's explanations and
interpretations. He was clearly impressed, too, by the
people Fidel had assembled around him. Raúl Castro
had already had a powerful impact on Che, and the urban
leader of the movement, Frank País, also impressed him
greatly. (Although it is not clear whether they met during
País's brief visits to Mexico, they did meet in 1957, not
long before País's death.)

País would be a key figure in the 26 July Movement, as
organiser of the urban movement. He attempted to dissuade Castro from launching the invasion, because the
urban organisation was not yet strong enough. Fine leader
though he was, País, a young teacher, was a very recent
recruit to the group. In the end, Castro convinced him of
the urgency of the plan.

José Antonio Echevarria, another visitor and leader of
the Directorio, was a key figure until his death in the failed
assassination attempt on Batista in 1957. Yet Castro was
extremely wary of the urban terrorism employed by the
group – and even publicly condemned the assassination of
one of Batista's key security service organisers. Given that
Fidel was planning to launch a guerrilla war, this seems
odd. On the other hand, Echevarria was a key political
rival, and Castro had no intention of sharing the leadership
of his armed force.[43]

Some historians[44] have added to the list of visitors to
the Cuban colony in Mexico the names of several important leaders of the Communist Party. The implication is
that they were in some way involved in Castro's coming
adventure. The greater likelihood is that they visited Castro to try to dissuade him from his plans and to accept
their leadership. Their later contemptuous comments on
Castro suggest that he rejected their overtures – as was

only to be expected from a man as arrogant, as ambitious and as virulently anti-Communist as the young ex-lawyer.

Late in 1955 the small group began its physical training. At first this involved long walks along the 17-mile avenue – Insurgentes – that crosses Mexico City. Later, the group tried to climb the conical volcano of Popocatépetl outside the city. Because of the shifting volcanic ash that covers the mountain, it is an exhausting ascent and Che's asthma stopped him from ever reaching the top. But he kept trying. There are photographs of the group rowing vigorously across the boating lake at the city's Chapultepec park. In February they began target practice at a suburban firing range. On 26 February Che's daughter Hilda Beatriz was born.

At this point, Alberto Bayo joined the group. He had been a colonel in the Republican army during the Spanish Civil War, and was a family contact of Fidel's. He agreed to help the group in their training, and hired a small and dilapidated farm near Chalco for the purpose.[45] Their activities lasted little more than a month. In mid-June the Mexican police arrested Castro and a number of others, and the Chalco camp was dismantled. Shortly afterwards, Che was arrested too.

It is hard to imagine how the motley crew at Chalco could become, within less than six months, a revolutionary army – or at least the nucleus of one. Yet it was during those weeks, and that rather amateurish training, that Ernesto Guevara became El Che, the expedition doctor. Even his speech began to change as he took on the Cuban accent and some Caribbean mannerisms.[46] He had begun to read his way into Marxist writings in a slightly more systematic way, though he was still prone to writing terrible mock-heroic poetry full of references to sacrifice and bravery. In the context of this group, however, he increasingly emerged as one of the more political. Taibo records a conversation at the camp which reveals how broad the range of ideas and attitudes was among those gathered under the umbrella of the 26 July Movement:

> It's simple really, he said. We've got to get in the first blow. That's how Batista managed to take power in one day, now we've got to do it to get rid of him. What mattered was taking power. I said that we had to make the move on the basis of principles, that the important thing was to know what we were going to do with power.[47]

The man Che was talking to eventually left the group – but he had been one of Fidel's companions in the Moncada assault, so he was not speaking for himself alone.

When Che found himself in jail alongside the Cubans, it seemed entirely logical that he should be there – although he also told Fidel not to worry about him, that he did not want the attempt to get him out of jail to jeopardise the plan. But Fidel did get him out – and Che was moved by the loyalty he saw in that gesture. In July he wrote to his parents to say:

> My future is tied in now with the Cuban revolution. I will triumph with it, or perish in the attempt.[48]

The die was cast. The training, brief and limited though it was, was over. In September Fidel bought a leaky old motorboat, the *Granma*, from an American expatriate for $40,000. The money came from an unlikely and highly suspect source – Prío Socarrás, the corrupt and unscrupulous previous president ousted by Batista.[49] Did Che know? It seems unlikely. He was at that time a fugitive, an illegal resident, having failed to leave Mexico within the ten days grace he had been given on leaving jail. Moving from safe house to safe house, he was taken slightly by surprise when Fidel called him and the others scattered around the country to assemble on 22 November in a house in Tuxpan, on the Gulf of Mexico.

On the night of 24 November, 82 men gathered around the *Granma*. Not all the volunteers were able to go. The boat was small and leaky, and the weather was brutal. It was raining, and winds lashed the coast and would continue to do so for the three days of the 80-mile journey. They left at 1.30 the next morning in silence – all you could hear were the dogs howling, Faustino Pérez remembered.

The three days became seven. The small boat and its unseaworthy crew were battered and blown off course again and again by the wind. Then, on the morning of 2 December 1956, they saw land. It was a place called Belic. They were two kilometres away from the beach where they intended to land. And they were expected.

As agreed, Frank País had organised a rising in the city of Santiago on 30 November, timed to coincide with the intended landing of the *Granma*.

A group of 27 armed men, for the first time wearing the emblems of the 26 July Movement, had taken to the streets at dawn. That evening they withdrew, leaving nine of their number dead. Brutal repression followed. Worse still, Batista's forces had been given a warning. Coastguard patrols were intensified and troops reinforced along the coast.

The voyage of the *Granma* had been a disaster. The boat was too small and fragile for a group of 82. Most were seasick and there were no pills for Che to distribute. He was very ill himself – he had left behind his inhaler in the rush to join the boat and his asthma immobilised him.

Celia Sánchez had been waiting with arms and extra people at the appointed place. After two days she assumed the plan had been aborted and left. When the expedition landed they discovered that the Belic headland was an entry to a mangrove swamp. They split into two groups, and struggled and stumbled through the labyrinth of tough mangled roots. Planes flew overhead, firing into the bush, throughout the two days of wandering before the two groups were reunited.

They were all exhausted when they reached the cane field at a place called Alegría del Pío. Their guide, a local peasant, disappeared while the guerrillas rested on the edge of the field. At around 4.30 in the afternoon the army attacked with support from the air. Che describes the desperate situation they were in:

> During the gun battle at Alegría del Pío a comrade dropped a cartridge box at my feet – it's too late for bullets, he said… For the first time I faced the dilemma of choosing between my dedication to medicine and my duty as a revolutionary soldier. At my feet were a pack of medicines and a cartridge box. Together they were too heavy to carry. I chose the bullets… Then I felt a terrible blow to the chest. I was sure I was dead.

In his field diary, Che says, 'I lost hope for a couple of minutes.' That moment of resignation does not appear in the published *Reminiscences*:

> Almeida urged me to move. The light planes flew low over us. The scene was grotesque – one stout guerrillero trying to hide behind a single sugar cane stalk, another crying out for silence amidst all this uproar…
>
> Reaching a small wood, we walked until night fell, then slept huddled together. We were attacked by mosquitoes, tortured by thirst and racked with hunger. This was the baptism of fire of the Rebel Army – on 5 December 1956.[50]

The next few days were a nightmare. The survivors had scattered across the countryside with the troops in pursuit. Che's group of five kept moving – they had scarcely any food or water. They felt, he said, 'like rats in a trap'. On 13 December a sympathetic farmer welcomed them in and they ate heartily for the first time in over a week – too heartily, as it turned out. Everyone in the group (there were eight of them now) was terribly sick.

Little by little they pieced together what had happened, although information was still fragmentary. A number of the *Granma* group had been killed either in exchanges of fire or immediately after their arrest. Some had escaped, Fidel among them.

Of the 82 men who had boarded the *Granma*, just 19 had survived. Another eight would join them later. In a curious twist, the most widely read account of the guerrilla campaign and its disastrous beginning is Carlos Franqui's *The Twelve*.[51] Why 12? It is impossible to ignore the deliberate religious overtones, the mythologising of the revolutionaries. The book was published after the victory of the revolution (in 1960). It tells us as much about how Castro wanted himself to be seen in the new Cuba as about the actual events of the guerrilla war.

On 21 December Che's group was reunited with Fidel. But it was not a particularly happy meeting. Fidel was furious because the fugitives had lost their weapons. It was a churlish reaction, and Che was deeply hurt by it, especially when Castro took away his pistol and replaced it with an old rifle – a deliberate humiliation. Che's hurt pride, however, did not dent his admiration for and loyalty to Fidel. It was an example of Fidel's arrogant machismo. But it may also have been a way of hiding from the others the obvious failure of the first invasion plan.

The *Granma* landing had been a disaster, and the

Santiago insurrection, courageous though it was, was an isolated and minority action. The 26 July Movement had supporters and sympathisers scattered across the island, but they were not connected with the trade unions or any other organisations outside their own circle. Yet it seems likely that Fidel had expected a general rising of the population. Now the scattered remnants of the group began to re-establish contact with Celia Sánchez and other supporters. It was clear, though, that a new strategy for a prolonged guerrilla war would have to emerge.

No guerrilla group (or *foco*, as Che would later describe it) could survive without the support of an urban movement. The relationship between mountain (*sierra*) and plain (*llano*) was at the heart of the political debates in the years that followed – above all, in the argument about which section should lead the movement.

For the moment, however, the small group simply survived through the New Year of 1957. Fidel was anxious that they should make their mark – and make it known in some spectacular way that they had survived the landing of the *Granma*. On 17 January the opportunity came.

Chicho Osorio was a notorious local political boss. Finding themselves on his estate, the guerrillas took on his guards and assassinated the hated Osorio. It was hardly a model operation. The pins on two grenades stuck, and a stick of dynamite failed to explode. Nonetheless the guerrillas had survived and made their first impact. In retrospect Che's manuals give the impression of considered tactical decisions.[52] In fact this was hardly a highly trained and well organised force. At this stage, things were happening in impromptu ways, and a great deal was down to luck.

Che Guevara with Raúl and Fidel Castro, Havana, 1960

Osvaldo Salas

7 | La sierra y el llano: the mountain and the plain

The group moved on, pursued by the army. At this stage, Che's key concern was the activity of informers, the chivatos who kept the army appraised of the movements of the guerrillas. Their activity kept the guerrillas on the move and in constant danger, and Che was unforgiving in his treatment of them. In a confrontation with Batista's troops a few days later, Che killed for the first time. Hearing that a deserter from their group had been tortured and killed by the army, Che commented that it was 'sad but instructive'.[53] When Eutimio Guerra, who had betrayed the group, was caught, it was Che who executed him with a pistol shot. His account of the execution is full of an odd kind of moral intensity, but he expresses neither pain nor regret. Everything indicated that Che was living through important psychological changes:

> Ernesto Che Guevara was now at war, trying to create a revolution, the result of a conscious leap of faith.[54]

The wild and reckless youth was becoming a harder, more determined and more disciplined person, convinced that a tough fighting force had to be remorseless in its internal discipline. While he applied the same harsh rules to himself, this rigidity and insistence on internal regimentation could be read in two different ways. It was either evidence of the fragility of this force which depended, ultimately, on isolated poor farmers with little political tradition, or it was a sign of the emphasis placed by Che on military qualities rather than political conviction in the maintenance of a guerrilla army. Anderson describes it as a kind of 'Calvinism', a black and white vision of the world which would tolerate no vacillations or ambiguities, no positions in between.

Although Che was already occupying a central role in the military arena, he was not yet part of the political leadership of the 26 July Movement. His diaries and writings from this phase of the struggle resonate with moral fervour and an emphasis on courage and sacrifice. He makes very little reference, by contrast, to the wider movement on the island or the strategic questions it needed to face. He had no independent contact with the other elements of the opposition to Batista except through Fidel and Raúl, and he exhibited very limited knowledge of the complex internal relations and tensions within the movement.

The reality is that in his vision of the revolutionary war – a war conducted by revolutionaries *on behalf of* the masses – the state of the workers' movement or the mass urban resistance was not an essential issue. In Che's view, the heart of the struggle was in the guerrilla struggle in the mountains – *la sierra*. When the history of the pre-revolutionary struggles came to be written after 1959, the centrality of the mountains was taken wholly for granted. Yet in these first weeks of 1957, when the guerrillas were a scattered group, barely surviving and harassed and persecuted by the army, a political battle within the movement was already going on beneath the surface.

At one level, the argument concerned who should lead the movement – the guerrillas under Fidel, or the urban movement, or the Directorio, or the Communists. More profoundly, the issue was who should conduct the guerrilla war – indeed, who were the guerrillas, beyond the small self-selecting group who had landed from the *Granma*? Was a guerrilla army a working-class militia, consisting essentially of armed and organised workers? Was it a force that drew together agricultural workers (and in Cuba that meant principally the cane cutters) and small farmers or peasants to fight a war of position in the countryside? Here Che and Fidel were in agreement, though almost certainly for different reasons.

The guerrilla war would be fought in the Sierra Maestra, an inhospitable mountain region where Batista's troops were restricted in their movements and limited in their response to guerrilla actions. The inhabitants of the area were mainly isolated and very poor farmers who were both physically and socially remote from the centres of collective organisation in the cities or the large farms and plantations. They certainly hated the Batista regime, which for them was largely represented by the arbitrary power of local politicians and an oppressive central state which offered them little or nothing in the way of support. They might be persuaded to join the army for those reasons, or at least to offer the guerrilla fighters support. On the other hand, as soon became clear, they were by no means automatically convinced by the new arrivals – and often fearful of the revenge the state would wreak upon them if their links with the rebels were discovered.

In another sense, the argument over whether the focus

of the struggle should be the *llano* – literally the plains, but also a reference to the cities – or the *sierra*, was actually a debate over *who* should lead the opposition to Batista. A programme for seizing power necessarily carries within it, in one form or another, the seeds of the kind of society that will emerge when and if power is taken.

News that an American journalist, Herbert Matthews, who worked for the prestigious *Life* magazine, wanted to interview Fidel came at a very opportune moment – and Fidel exploited the opportunity to the full.

The timing of the interview, in February 1957, coincided with the first meeting between the national directorate of the 26 July Movement and Fidel since the *Granma* landing.

The reality was that Fidel probably had just 17 guerrillas around him at this time. While their presence in the mountains was common knowledge, their military impact had been minimal. In the cities the M-26-J did enjoy some support, but the failed attempt at an uprising in Santiago just three months earlier had revealed how small it was – and how student-based. It had failed, as yet, to win any significant support among organisations of workers.[55]

On the morning of 17 February Herbert Matthews was brought to Fidel's camp. Meticulous preparations were made to give Matthews the best possible impression of the Movement. Halfway through the interview, for example, a fighter came in panting with a message from a (fictitious) second column. Fidel was also careful to avoid any easy political labels. When the journalist asked whether he was anti-imperialist, Fidel evaded the question. Matthews was impressed:

> The personality of the man is overpowering. It was easy to see that his men adored him and also to see why he has

caught the imagination of the youth of Cuba all over the island... The program is vague and couched in generalities, but it amounts to a new deal for Cuba, radical, democratic and therefore anti-Communist.[56]

It was a massive publicity coup against Batista, who had announced Castro's death and the destruction of the guerrilla army several times in the preceding days. Earl T Smith, the US ambassador and a close ally of Batista, was understandably enraged by the *Life* reports. They seemed to him to indicate waning support for the friends of the US interest in Cuba.[57]

Che was not present at the Matthews interview and was not aware of how Fidel intended to exploit the moment. This seems surprising, given the central role that Che would play in the revolution both before and after Batista's overthrow. And he was, after all, the expedition doctor – a pivotal function in itself. On the other hand, he was not a member of the national directorate. Perhaps he was still paying for what Fidel considered to be his serious error at Alegría del Pío? A more plausible explanation might be found in the political crossroads at which the M-26-J now found itself, a crossroads at which Fidel intended to reaffirm his uncontested leadership of the revolution.

Che records in his diary that it was on this occasion he met the key leaders of the Movement[58] for the first time – the lawyer Armando Hart, the brilliant Frank País, Haydée Santamaría, who had joined the Moncada assault with her brother (he was killed during the action),[59] Vilma Espín, Raúl Castro's future wife, and, of course, Celia Sánchez. All of them had emerged from the student movement. In his unpublished diaries Che expressed some concern at their shared middle-class background. He was also more than a little surprised at the limited political horizons of many of them. They were anti-Communists and nationalists – but not socialists or revolutionaries.[60]

The meeting of the national directorate continued until the following day. Frank País argued in favour of building an urban resistance movement and suggested that Fidel might follow up on the Matthews interview with a solidarity tour outside Cuba. Faustino Pérez argued for the opening of a second front in Escambray. It seems possible, too, that Raúl was building his contacts with the Communists and probably argued for developing these links as a priority.

Matthews was right about Castro's charismatic personality. By the end of the meeting of the directorate, Fidel had imposed his political vision. The building of the rebel army was to be the absolute priority, and a call was to be issued for the organisation of a 'civic resistance' whose essential function was to *support* the guerrilla fighters, materially and with spectacular actions of sabotage. Fidel's manifesto also claimed that the rebel army was steadily growing – which was simply untrue. In fact, the brutal reprisals meted out to anyone who helped the rebels isolated the guerrillas even more from the local peasantry. Yet the political balance within the resistance had tipped definitively Castro's way by the end of the meeting, and against the urban representatives like Carlos Franqui, editor of the Movement's journal *Revolución* (the people Che had described as 'anti-Communists'). When Franqui published a manifesto in late February which described the movement as 'democratic, nationalist and socialist', Castro was quick to repudiate the description. Franqui also expressed at the time a concern that Fidel was becoming an increasingly authoritarian leader – a *caudillo* in the language of Latin American politics.[61]

Events early in March reinforced the structures of command. On 13 March the failed assassination attempt against

Batista effectively destroyed the Directorio, and the death of its leader Echevarría removed the most significant challenger to Castro's base among students and youth.

Fidel withdrew into the Sierra Maestra. Che began the journey with him, but by the end of February his asthma was crippling. It was decided he should stay behind and wait for the new recruits from the city, as well as new supplies of adrenalin. The rebel army was now approaching 80 men. No doubt Matthews's recently published interview, which had caused a furore, acted as a recruiting sergeant. So, too, did the collapse of the Directorio. To compound matters, Frank País and Armando Hart, key leaders of the urban movement, were arrested after a failed attempt to plant a bomb in Camaguey.

When Che and Fidel's groups met up again, Fidel was bitterly critical of Che for failing to impose his authority on the new urban recruits and their leader, Sotús. Despite Raúl's attempts to persuade his brother that Che should be given a leading political role, Fidel effectively demoted him again.

Yet Che did not protest. In the protean world of heroes and moral certainties in which he lived, each affirmation of authority by Fidel produced new admiration in Che. By contrast he was contemptuous of the urban warriors of the Directorio. Perhaps Anderson is right to suggest that for Che, until then the radical individualist, what mattered most at this moment was the group, the fellow feeling of the band of rebels. Although Che was developing a general political view, it was also plain that his judgements about things were first and foremost moral judgements. His yardsticks were loyalty, courage, selflessness and technical preparedness. He had none of the guile and the capacity for instant adaptation that marked Fidel's political career. The effect of Che's personal qualities on others, however, was to inspire the same responses in them. Though Fidel was abrasive with him, his other comrades cared deeply for the Argentine medic who smoked cigars to keep the mosquitoes away, and whose beard (now obligatory for the revolutionaries) never seemed to get beyond the wispy stage.

However, it was clear that Che and Fidel were in agreement about the tactics the guerrilla army should now follow. In his handbook for guerrillas – *Guerrilla Warfare* – Che coined the notion of 'armed propaganda'. The actions of the rebel army are not in the first place designed to achieve a straightforward military victory, but rather to undermine and demoralise the state's forces by exposing their weakness. The other face of this, of course, is to exalt and celebrate the achievements of the rebels – to create a myth of invincibility, of cunning and subtle manoeuvre.

If the rebels were to justify their reputation, an armed action was now urgent. On 28 May six rebels died in an attack on an army barracks at Uvero. At one point Che, feeling the battle was going badly, stood up and advanced, firing his gun and shouting, 'We must win.' This act of folly and unthinking spontaneity won Fidel's admiration and approval. Che was left to oversee the journey of the wounded, while Fidel withdrew again into the mountains. Che's party moved very slowly, and the local population proved to be less than enthusiastic about helping the wounded guerrillas.

When Fidel and Che finally met up again on 17 July, Che was faced with an unpalatable reality. Once again the calculating pragmatism of Castro clashed with the idealism and conviction that impelled Che forward in the struggle. While Che was making his slow way back, Fidel had been holding talks with two representatives of the old Ortodoxo party, to which he had once belonged. One was

Raúl Chibas, brother of the dead Eduardo, the other Felipe Pazos, ex-governor of Cuba's National Bank. In fact Castro had signed and already published an agreement with them ahead of the recently announced 1958 presidential elections.

It was a pact with a group of deeply compromised right-wing politicians. Che distrusted these 'prima donnas of the moment' as he called them, and with every reason – he was deeply suspicious of their involvement with the Movement. They were certainly opposed to Batista, but for their own opportunistic reasons. They could not be regarded as political allies of a revolutionary movement, at least not beyond the expedient present. Che's diary records long discussions with Fidel, who convinced him that he had intended to produce a 'really militant document' which was blocked by these 'stone-age brains'.[62] In the end Che was convinced. But here, not for the first or last time, pragmatism and idealism clashed.

The reality was that the Movement in the cities had suffered a series of blows. Carlos Franqui had been arrested and, of the urban network, only Celia was still free after the arrests of País and Hart. Within weeks the acknowledged leader of the 26 July Movement in the cities, Frank País, was dead.

Perhaps this was what persuaded Che grudgingly to accept the necessity of what came to be called the Miami Pact with Chibas and Pazos. He remained unhappy about it. But his reasons were in some senses contradictory. While he was opposed in principle to pacts with corrupt, liberal politicians, he was also disturbed by Fidel's apparent willingness to abandon key points in the programme in order to placate them. The agrarian reform provision, for example, was now amended to include the right to compensation of the landowners – an obvious concession to

Fidel's new allies. Che knew enough about the attitudes of the peasant farmers to be certain that this would never win their support.

On the other hand, he identified urban politics (the *llano*) with reformism and the politics of the guerrillas in the hills (the *sierra*) with revolution. Che spoke about the city as an undifferentiated place. In fact, his dismissal of the urban struggle effectively marginalised trade unions and workers too. Yet the *sierra* was not rural Cuba, where a class of peasant farmers and agricultural workers might have been seen as an alternative base for a revolutionary movement. These sections of Cuban society lived on the 'plains' (the *llano*) too. Che (and Fidel) meant the more remote and difficult terrain of the Sierra Maestra – ideal for a cat-and-mouse military strategy, but not a region whose sparse and scattered population could build a social movement. The strategy that Che and Fidel had in common envisaged a guerrilla war conducted by small groups of revolutionary fighters rather than by the masses in whose name they claimed to be waging the struggle.

After País's murder, Che engaged in a lengthy correspondence with 'Daniel' (René Lamos Latour) in which Daniel angrily repudiated Che's simplistic view of the battle on the 'plains'. As far as Che was concerned, it was the revolutionaries who carried through the revolution in the name of and on behalf of the people. Daniel retorted that, even if the work in the city did not offer as many heroic opportunities, those who sustained the guerrillas in the city were just as courageous. But he did not really challenge Che's view *politically*.

There were clear reasons in Che's background to explain this relegation of the working class and the small farmers to a position of support for the guerrillas. Indeed, it was one of the original points of agreement between Fidel and himself when they met in Mexico. Fidel's hostility to the socialist political tradition which was rooted in the idea of workers' power was explicit and well documented (Che described it as the movement's 'anti-Communism').

So on the one hand, Che placed himself alongside Raúl Castro (the closest of all the 26 July leaders to the Communist Party) in his criticism of this Miami Pact. On the other, his alternative was revolutionary idealism and moral purity, rather than work with wider social forces that could make the revolution. He remained an unconditional admirer and follower of Fidel for that very reason.

On 21 July Che was finally made a 'comandante' – although the promotion was slightly tainted by the fact that Raúl was simultaneously demoted to lieutenant for reasons never made clear, but which might well have had to do with arguments over the Miami Pact. Perhaps Fidel was simply moving his pieces around the chessboard again.

There were now increasing signs that Washington was beginning to turn against its old ally Batista – whose repressive state and transparent corruption were becoming an embarrassment, especially now that a political alternative was acquiring an increasing public profile. The new US ambassador, Earl Smith, once the stoutest of Batista's defenders, now made public reference to the use of torture by the police during his inaugural tour of the island. And the CIA was opening contact with the opposition to the dictatorship. Reformist officers in the navy, for example, were planning a coup in the port of Cienfuegos to coincide with similar actions by opponents in the army and air force. The CIA promised its support if that happened.

Much to Che's alarm, the 26 July Movement was also in regular contact with the CIA. Frank País, just before his death, had been corresponding with Fidel about a possible meeting with CIA agents, and money had already reached the Movement from US government agencies. País had also proposed a new structure for the Movement which would have given each of its areas of activity equal representation in the leadership. However, Fidel considered himself to be the sole and unquestioned leader of the opposition to Batista – an opposition that was undoubtedly growing on several fronts.

The Cienfuegos attack went ahead on 5 September 1957. But the simultaneous risings expected in Havana and Santiago did not happen and Batista concentrated all his firepower on crushing the rebellion. The repression was barbaric. Some 300 conspirators were murdered, many of them tortured first.[63] So savage was Batista's response that the number of those in Washington who saw him as a liability began to grow. The effect of the Cienfuegos repression and the death of Frank País confirmed Fidel in the leadership of the rebellion.

Where did Che stand in all this? The debate with 'Daniel' left little room for doubt. Che was not just a committed guerrilla and a military organiser – he was also a political leader of the 26 July Movement whose views and beliefs coincided with Fidel's. But he was deeply uneasy about Castro's deals and manoeuvres with right-wing politicians, the CIA and the Miami Mafia – and he expressed his discomfort in his field diaries.[64] He had already voiced his suspicion of what he called the 'anti-Communists' of M-26-J. Yet these people came from the same background, politically speaking, as Fidel and shared the same deep hostility towards the corrupt and compromised Cuban Communist Party. By now Che considered himself a Marxist, and provided education in basic Marxism to the recruits he trained. This certainly brought him closer to Raúl Castro, who of all the leaders of the Movement was in most regular contact with the Communists. Yet Che was equally critical of a Communism that had betrayed its most fundamental principles – and this tension would become more apparent as, during the 1960s, the contradictions and betrayals of the 'official' Communism of Eastern Europe were steadily revealed.

In his politics as well as his revolutionary commitment, Che was uncompromising. But for him the instrument of revolutionary change was the rebel army, and its method was guerrilla warfare. Che's manual for mountain fighters, *Guerrilla Warfare*, was not, therefore, just a logistical, military document – it was also a political one. It argued that the revolutionary war would be won or lost according to the degree of technical preparation, military expertise and, above all, *discipline* in the revolutionary cell or *foco*. Hence the jarring fact that Che was extremely harsh with his own men and with anyone who endangered the cause, deliberately or otherwise. He readily executed informers and deserters, yet was magnanimous with enemy soldiers. This was a response that could only have arisen out of a military code of honour.

Che looked to the workers' movement, students and protest only to support and supply the guerrillas. He described himself as a Marxist now. Yet for Marx, a revolution was the moment when the working class achieved its own liberation through collective action. This does not appear in Che's worldview – or in his political writings – any more than it does in the political pronouncements and manifestos of Castro.

Che Guevara and Fidel Castro inspecting workplaces after the revolution, Havana, 1960

Osvaldo Salas

8 | The short march to Havana

In September Guevara established a permanent encampment at El Hombrito. It had a small armoury, a cigar-making workshop and a radio receiver which began broadcasting in February 1958. Che described the area under guerrilla control as a 'liberated zone' and painted a utopian picture of life there. Che's young recruits were mainly from the surrounding area, and very new to the Marxist ideas that Che summarised for them at impromptu seminars. Indeed, both Che and Fidel seemed to suggest that these ideas did not exist in Cuban political culture, but that was to underestimate the influence of Communists and other revolutionary socialists with a long if chequered involvement in Cuban politics.[66]

By the end of 1957 the guerrillas and the Cuban state had reached a kind of stand-off. Two new fronts had been established, though the reality was much less impressive than the rhetoric. These fronts comprised small groups of guerrillas established to begin the accumulation of forces. By and large the army had kept away from the mountain areas.

Guevara's own balance sheet of 1957[68] was relentlessly positive (as was Fidel's):

> By the end of this first year of struggle, a generalised uprising throughout the country was looming on the horizon.[69]

He was, I think, exaggerating for effect. There was no doubt that the guerrilla army had made its mark – and had won the sympathy of a majority of Cubans. Batista's repression and persecution of anyone it thought might have supported the Movement won it only a growing number of enemies – and an increasing coolness on the part of Washington. New recruits were joining the guerrillas in the mountains. On the other hand, the urban movement had suffered major and terrible defeats, beginning with the murder of Frank País and the failure of the Camaguey rising.

The debates between Che and Daniel[70] were one echo of the internal arguments that had arisen in the attempt to understand the gulf between the two experiences. In Che's view the movement in the cities had failed, and this was a vindication of the strategy that he and Fidel put forward, which focused on armed struggle. When he described life in the 'liberated zones', he was at pains to stress how people changed there – and change in Che's view began with participation in the armed struggle. So he could say, for example:

> I once made an observation to a PSP leader, which he later repeated to others as an accurate characterisation of that period: 'You are capable of creating cadres who can silently endure the most terrible tortures in jail, but you cannot create cadres who can take a machine-gun nest'.[71]

At every turn, Che's emphasis was on the commitment and determination of the revolutionaries. There was no assessment of social forces, no discussion of how to build a mass movement or of the relationship between the rebel army and that wider movement. The mountains, after all, were a military location. Politics – the plains – were always to be subordinate to it.

For revolutionary socialists, a revolutionary process is one in which people become involved directly in shaping their own destiny, and it is the experience of becoming an active agent that will shape the new – socialist – society that emerges. Socialism is not a matter of changing leaders, but of building a society based on different values (production for need not profit, for example). It involves a completely different view of what democracy means – direct day-to-day involvement in shaping society rather than the occasional vote for one or other self-selected politician.

As 1958 began, Che and Fidel continued to be embroiled in a bitter political fight for their conception of how the revolutionary war should be waged. Surprisingly, perhaps – given Fidel's enduring suspicions – contacts with the Cuban Communist Party were prospering and there was regular traffic between the city and the mountains. Some leading Communists were joining Fidel's troops, and contacts between their organisations were developing fast. This reflected the deteriorating relations between the Communists and the 26 July Movement in the cities. It was clear that the PSP's new enthusiasm for the guerrillas had more than a little to do with a desire to drive a wedge between the Movement's two sections.

In March 1958 the Catholic church sponsored a peace initiative – and the courts seemed ready to condemn Batista's henchmen and thugs. The dictator responded by postponing elections scheduled for June and launching a new wave of repression. The Movement responded with a call for what it called 'total war' against the regime – beginning with a general strike on 9 April. It was a disastrous failure. The unions did not respond and the PSP, spurned by the Movement's urban leadership, turned its back on the whole thing.

In the aftermath, the 26 July Movement made a decisive political turn. On 3 May the national directorate met in the Sierra Maestra. Reporting later, Che said:

> The meeting discussed and passed judgement on two conceptions that had clashed with one another throughout the whole previous stage of directing the war. The guerrilla conception would emerge triumphant from that meeting. Fidel's standing and authority were consolidated.[72]

It was not just that command was now solely concentrated in the hands of Fidel, with Che's unconditional support. The structure of the movement was now shaped by the military struggle.

For his part, Che had reached the conclusions he would later develop in *Guerrilla Warfare*. First, that a popular army can win a military struggle against a regular army. Second, that in the particular conditions of Latin America it is the poor peasants who are the most revolutionary class – rather than organised workers in industry or agriculture. Third, that the conditions for revolution do not need to exist before the struggle begins – the revolutionary *foco* can create them.[73]

Che's ideas would have repercussions he could not have dreamed of. They would shape the future struggles of a whole generation of young revolutionaries in Latin America in a way that would have terrible and long-term consequences.

In a way, Che was reacting against a certain pessimistic gradualism he had heard from other socialists – the notion that 'objective conditions' had to exist before change was possible, as if revolutionaries did not have an active role to play in bringing those conditions about. Yet in identifying the poor peasantry as the key social group in the revolution, Che was specifically rejecting Marxism's central idea – that it is the power of the organised working class alone that can bring about a social revolution. Some countries in Latin America were still dominated by small-scale agricultural production – and the argument that the peasantry was a revolutionary class still had some weight in those circumstances. But like his own country, Argentina, or Mexico – where he had spent a great deal of time – Cuba was integrated into an international economy as a mono-producer of sugar and was already highly urbanised.

Che's conception of revolution only acknowledged the role of those who carried the arms and did the fighting. They alone were the revolutionary actors. What of the urban workers, the students, the people in the small towns? Their task was to supply the fighters and support them. And if that was how the revolution was to be made, then it was also how the society which emerged from the revolution would be. The revolutionaries would command and the majority would offer support to those who fought on their behalf. In a military structure there could be neither democracy nor transparency – both could spell disaster in a military context. But in a society, their absence would be a disaster.

Although Fidel and Che could not know it at the time, by May the Batista regime was losing support from its masters in Washington and starting to crumble from within.[74] Of course, the US government had not suffered some collective crisis of conscience. Its other favourite dictatorships were still firmly established in Nicaragua, Guatemala, Peru and so on. This was still the period of the Cold War in which every movement for freedom, national independence or social justice was interpreted by the US State Department as evidence of Communist influence.

But US domination in the region was not in question, only the ability of the deeply unpopular Batista regime to successfully defend US interests against a broad, popular opposition. And that opposition was growing.

After the failure of the April strikes, Batista threw massive numbers of troops against the guerrillas. By the end of the first week of May 1958 there were 10,000 government troops surrounding the rebels. Despite the US's public refusal to give arms to Batista, US missiles were used in air raids on villages and encampments at the entrance to the mountains.

Through all this, Che was based at the training camp of Minas del Frío, preparing new recruits who would later form the basis of a second front in the east. It was a key task, but frustrating for Che. He had hoped to take part in the battles with the army, alongside his friend Camilo Cienfuegos. But while Fidel was largely static at the command centre, Che became effectively a second in command, running the all-important radio and communications networks. While it might seem these were secondary tasks at such moments of confrontation, the impact of the rebels was multiplied and expanded through these communications with the world beyond the sierra. It helped to create the impression of a much larger and more powerful organisation than the one that actually existed.

What was the reality of the rebel forces at this point? Fidel had some 280 soldiers with him with about 50 rounds of ammunition each. Raúl's second front, in the Sierra de Cristal, probably comprised about 200 fighters. Both groups were besieged and encircled by Batista's ground and air offensive:

> That circle was never that wide to begin with. The entire rebel stronghold…was actually only a tiny area of a few square miles. The distance between Fidel's comandancia and the northern frontline village of Las Mercedes was 12 kilometres, and the recruits school at Minas del Frío sat halfway between them. To the south, less than eight kilometres from the rebel headquarters, lay the coast.[75]

Within the siege cracks were appearing, especially among the new recruits around Che. There were a number of escapes, and a rumbling discontent exacerbated and underlined by the regular bombing raids that hit the rebels through early June. If the troops held together at all, it was clearly due in good part to Che's personal qualities as a commander. On the one hand, he was energetic and courageous to the point of recklessness. He was honest with his people, and visibly willing to do what he asked others to do. On the other hand, he was remorseless with those he felt had betrayed or threatened the cause. There were several executions, and punishments were unstinting. One student who had panicked and tried to escape was sentenced to ten days without food. The fear, the desertions, the desperation were not hard to understand in a volunteer force under constant siege. Yet to those around him, Che Guevara appeared to have no fear of death.

By late June the tightening circle of besiegers had almost reached Fidel's command centre at La Plata. The outer columns of the 26 July Movement had drawn back, with the exception of Raúl's Sierra Cristal column. The number of desertions was rising and the siege continued. But the attack by Batista's troops was now in its third month. Two thirds of the government troops were conscripts. Some had crossed over to the rebel side. Those who remained were exhausted, many were wounded, and the terrain on which they were fighting seemed as much their enemy as the men in olive green who were alternately shooting and shouting at them through megaphones across the echoing passes. Demoralisation was the greatest ally of the rebels.

When Raúl's column took 46 Americans hostage, Fidel was not particularly pleased. The week or so it took to negotiate their release was a time of recovery for Raúl's fighters. But it somewhat undermined Fidel's careful efforts to court US public opinion. Early that month, for example, Fidel had signed an agreement in Caracas with the other Cuban opposition group, but had not included the Cuban Communists. In fact, there were Communists in the sierra speaking with Fidel at the time, but he was anxious not to make this public. Che found this perplexing – Fidel had not shared his plans with him.

Late in July the tide began to turn. The rebels captured a number of Batista's soldiers and besieged several of his companies. By 7 August the army was moving – or stumbling – out of the mountains. While sporadic air attacks began again some days later, the rebel army had survived.

It was imperative now to seize the brief advantage and expand the range of battle by opening a second front in the east. The task fell to Che – and this would nourish his status as a legend among the rebels. Fidel's nomination of Che for this task was a mark of his respect and regard for the Argentine. Yet while the two men were wholly in agreement on the military strategy, and in their suspicion of some of the members of their own movement in the cities, there were differences between them that would re-emerge once both were in government.

These centred on their respective attitudes to the United States and to the Cuban Communists. The Caracas Pact had made very clear that Fidel saw the growing distance between the US government and Batista as a key factor in the situation – and he was quick to block any move which might allow conservatives in the US to characterise the 26 July Movement as Communist. Hence the exclusion of the PSP from the Caracas Pact, and Fidel's swift moves to return the hostages taken earlier by Raul. There have been endless debates ever since about whether Fidel was a secret Communist deliberately pretending to be a revolutionary nationalist. The reality is that his relationship with the Communists, now and well into the period of revolutionary government, was pragmatic rather than principled. For a very long time it was fraught and difficult.

Che, on the other hand, while fiercely critical of the Cuban Communists in many respects, described himself as a Communist. He supported the Soviet Union and saw Cuba's future in relation to the Eastern European bloc of countries. Yet as the revolution evolved, Che would become increasingly critical of the Soviet model while Fidel would become the leader and symbol of Cuban Communism.

At this point, however, Che's sympathy for the Communists, together with his personal qualities, were key to the task Fidel entrusted to him. Not only was it imperative to open another front, Che was also charged with uniting the several factions and groups fighting their own small guerrilla wars in the Escambray area.

The decision signalled a change in military tactics. Castro claimed the war was now moving from a guerrilla phase of fast-moving flexible units exposing the weakness of its enemy, into a war of position with several battlefronts on which the armies of the dictatorship would be engaged. Fidel now made the slogan of the French revolutionary Danton – 'Audacity, audacity and more audacity' – his own. Given the level of armaments and personnel at his disposal, it was an ambitious plan to say the least. But the key elements were not military but political – the defeat of the Batista assault on the Sierra Maestra, the growing unease among the dictator's political masters in Washington, and the popular revulsion at the corrupt and violent regime. Within Oriente province itself, the mere survival of the second front under Raúl was a kind of victory.

Fidel now publicly announced the 'invasion' of the rest of the island – and it was Che who would carry this through.

On 30 August 1958 Che set out for the centre of the island. His comrade Camilo Cienfuegos had already left for the far west, Pinar del Rio, with 82 men to set up a new front. Che followed with 142 in his column. He anticipated that four days would be enough to reach the Escambray mountains in Las Villas province in the central region. But disaster struck at the very outset. The petrol supplies and two of the lorries were lost in a battle with the Cuban army. The two remaining trucks were destroyed in a sudden cyclone that left them sunk into the mud and useless. The four days became a harsh 42-day trek through mud and rain. In the course of that 'long march' the legend of Che Guevara was definitively born.

It is doubtful whether anyone with less strength of character, less determination and less respect from those around him could have completed this painful route march. Those who followed Che were not hardened fighters but new young recruits, students and peasants, with minimum experience. If he dragged them through those 300 exhausting kilometres of swamp and mountain, it was testimony to his authority and his example. But Che was also intransigent – he did not forgive weakness (that had already been obvious to the recruits at the guerrilla training school at Minas) and he was remorseless when any of those he commanded made mistakes or misjudgements.

> He could not tolerate errors in his subordinates: he scolded, insulted and punished them… Che's decency (and nobility) always led him to apologise after a few hours or days. And he never demanded of his subordinates anything that he would not impose on himself. But these abstract qualities irritated people in the real world: others did not share his sense of destiny, intellect or willpower.[76]

Yet others did admire those qualities – and rely on them to overcome hostile material conditions. It made Che a great military leader. And it was clearly these challenges, these extreme demands which brought him the greatest sense of personal achievement. It is interesting, for example, that Che's diaries make no mention of his asthma at these times – the very conditions under which it might expected to flare up. It is as if the adrenalin rush, the excitement of these times was enough to suppress his asthma.

> The enemy is clearly identified, things are clear, the comrades are absolutely dedicated; he is at peace with himself and he has discovered that the best cure for his asthma is…the smell of gunpowder.[77]

For Che this was the first opportunity to take direct and independent command, with the full support of Castro.

Not only was his selflessness and steely courage a guarantee that he would fulfil this crucial project – he was also more likely to win over the other groups in the area. Castro may have grandiloquently described it as an invasion. The reality was that the most important achievement he could anticipate would simply be reaching the centre of the island, escaping the encirclement of Oriente province, and establishing a presence in the area around the capital, Havana.

This Guevara achieved, and the journey was made all the more dramatic by the repeated declarations of the local military commander, Lieutenant Colonel Suárez Suquet, that Guevara had fallen into his hands with documents proving his Communist affiliation.

The nightmare journey ended on 16 October 1958. Che now faced two urgent tasks. The first was to establish a unity of purpose between the squabbling factions in the Escambray hills. The second was to organise and encourage the boycott of the national elections called by Batista for 3 November. The election had really been forced on the dictator by the US, in the hope that an acceptable bourgeois alternative to Batista could be found and provide a limited change which might satisfy an increasingly discontented Cuban population. If the 26 July Movement was to maintain its political domination of the opposition to the dictatorship, it was imperative that the limited and basically fraudulent nature of the elections be exposed.

In the first of these tasks, Che proved to be skilled and politically independent. Among the groups in Escambray were two feuding units that had emerged from the urban wing of the Movement which had made the attempt on Batista's life two years earlier. In addition, the Cuban Communist Party had its own grouping in the area. The Communists were the first to make contact with Che, through Ovidio Díaz Rodríguez who was 26 years old and led the Las Villas Socialist Youth organisation. Guevara's reputation had preceded him, and Ovidio expressed his excitement at meeting the man who was already legend.

He found Che open and sympathetic, as did another leading PSP cadre who was sent to work with Che on propaganda and communication tasks. Che was sympathetic to Communism in general, but not to the Cuban Communist Party in particular. He had absorbed Fidel's deep suspicion of the PSP, a suspicion shared by many of the 26 July people, and particularly the young engineer of Polish extraction, Enrique Oltuski, who led their military unit. He was happy enough to work with Che, although he would not approve Che's plan for a bank robbery in the town of Sancti Spiritus. But he refused to work with Communists.

While looking for ways to unify these hostile groups, Che recognised the more urgent need was to start military activity in preparation for the November elections. However, his first act as commander of the region was to enact an agrarian reform decree, following the revolutionary law already announced by Castro in the Sierra Maestra. At this stage it was essentially a propaganda exercise, given the limited amount of land under the control of the rebel army. There was disagreement, however, about how far it should go. For Castro, the reform should be limited to the redistribution of land belonging to Batista and to other unused land in the area. Che was adamant that reform should mean taking on the big estates, immediately suspending rent payments and redistributing the land without promise of compensation. The PSP agreed with him.

Relations with the Communists continued to be tense and difficult. The PSP had, after all, denounced the armed struggle strategy of the 26 July Movement as 'adventurist'.

Yet Fidel was clearly interested in creating links of some kind. His brother Raúl was very close to the Communists and, in Escambray, Che was working with them. The people closest to Fidel, however, were highly suspicious of these exploratory moves and persuaded him to expel the PSP representative, Carlos Rafael Rodríguez, from his camp. Che disagreed, and when the attack on Guinía in Las Villas was being prepared, the PSP agreed to participate while the Directorio refused. There was still jealousy and competition between the local units.

Guevara would have none of it. He launched a series of small-scale actions while the other groups held. He had come with a strategic vision of a coordinated national movement and, one by one, he reached agreement with the different factions while insisting that he retained general command. Early in December the Pedrero Pact marked an agreement with the Directorio.

Large-scale abstention in the elections on 3 November strengthened the resolve of the fighters, and a series of small but significant successes fuelled their confidence. Roads and transport links were regularly cut, prisoners taken and arms captured. The coordination within Che's area and between his and Camilo's columns in the northern part of the province were reaping success. And amid all this, Guevara had found a new lover. A 22 year old activist who had taken refuge in El Pedrero, Aleida March would become his constant companion and bear him four children.

From Batista's point of view the November elections were the beginning of the end. Only 30 percent of the electorate voted, and in some places no more than 10 percent went to the polls. Che's unifying presence in the Escambray mountains was certainly an important factor in this popular rejection of the dictator. But subsequent histories of the struggle that represent him as the sole actor in these events are deeply misleading. The truth is that, despite the disaster of the April strike, the 26 July Movement's sections in the mountains had maintained their networks of support in some of the towns and rural areas in the centre of the island. The workers of one small tobacco factory, for example, sold their tobacco quota and sent the money to the guerrillas.[78] The Directorio Revolucionario units, with whom Che obviously felt some sympathy, also had a presence and a credibility rooted in their past actions.

Castro was concerned that these connections were too close. He had always seen the Directorio as his closest political competition, and thus worthy of suspicion and hostility. At the same time, Fidel was clearly keeping open channels of communication with the Communists, despite the hostility of his fellow leaders on the national directorate. The long-established hostility between the Directorio and the PSP could certainly have compromised those negotiations. Fidel was content to hold a line between the two.

The major factor in this changing situation, however, was objective. The failure of the elections, the success of small-scale but well publicised guerrilla actions in the area, the increasing brutality of Batista and the growing alienation of the population that it produced, had accelerated the collapse of the regime – particularly as increasing numbers of conscript soldiers gave up the fight. This became obvious as the battle proceeded through December and brought the guerrilla fighters closer and closer to Cuba's fourth city – the capital of Las Villas province, Santa Clara.

On 27 December Che approached the city. Both he and Fidel knew the fall of Batista would be determined here – so did the dictator. Che now commanded some 340 fighters. Batista's troops amounted to at least 4,000, and an armoured train full of weapons was on its way to reinforce the garrisons there. Santa Clara was a main rail and transport junction at the centre of the island – it was, in a sense, the gateway to Havana (although the port town of Matanzas lay between it and the capital).

The three days of battle were bitter and costly. But at a key moment the train was stopped on the outskirts of the city. The guerrillas had ripped up the rails, and the 22 coaches fell into a pile when they hit the broken track. Within a short time the soldiers on board surrendered. It was the last day of 1958.

In Havana, plots and counter-plots were hatched to try to stop the guerrillas. But treachery, corruption and betrayal are hard habits to break. Batista had his bags packed and his plans made. Late at night he excused himself from his New Year's Eve party guests and boarded a plane for the Dominican Republic – where fellow dictator Rafael Trujillo waited to welcome him.

9 | **Guerrillas in power**

On New Year's Day 1959 Cuba awoke to a future without Batista. In Santa Clara local militias guarded the soldiers who had spilled out of the armoured train and surrendered. There were still some snipers at police headquarters – Batista's most notorious torturers, who would find no place to hide in the city – and some of the dictator's security men, who held the central hotel. But just after midday the garrison surrendered and the population filled the streets, greeting the bearded men in olive green (*los barbudos*). By six o'clock that evening Santiago in the east had fallen to Castro.

On 2 January Camilo and Che led their columns the 300 kilometres to Havana. All along the highway they were cheered and applauded. At this moment, on these roads, Che Guevara was the hero of the hour, the mythic representative of a victorious guerrilla struggle. When the rebel column entered Havana the next day, however, it was led by Camilo Cienfuegos. Che arrived some hours later with a small party and under cover of night. Yet Camilo had until then functioned as Che's second in command – though his victory at Yaguajay, coinciding with the fall of Santa Clara, had been enormously significant. He was younger and, though a popular figure, his standing could not be compared with the heroic Argentine whose stamina, reckless bravery and complete neglect of himself and his own safety had already become the stuff of legend.

The instruction that Camilo should lead the victorious column had come from Fidel Castro, who was still in the eastern provinces but in charge of overall strategy. It had been demonstrated many times in the previous year that Che did not question the authority of Fidel. And it was always somewhere close to the forefront of Che's mind that he was, in the end, a foreigner without roots in Cuba. For ordinary Cubans, Che represented the physical reality of armed struggle, the qualities of the fighter, not the politician.

There was still more to it. Fidel had more than once expressed his unease at the links that Che had forged in the Escambray mountains with the Directorio fighters under Faure Chomón and with the PSP. It had been an absolute condition of the military victory of course. But Fidel's eyes were fixed on the question of political power. For him, it was imperative that the victory should be entirely credited to the 26 July Movement, that the organisation he led should be recognised unequivocally as the sole and commanding power in the new Cuba. By the time Fidel arrived in the capital, just under a week later, it must be as the uncontested leader of revolutionary Cuba.

Yet there was a contradiction here. The profile of the 26 July Movement that Castro led was at its highest because the victory over Batista was perceived as a *military* triumph. But Batista would not have fallen under the impact of the guerrilla attacks alone, however courageous and well organised they might have been. The dictator's masters in Washington had effectively withdrawn their support. There was an arms embargo in place, even if Batista had easy access to other sources. The army had disintegrated at the end. There was resistance and revulsion at the increasing repression and violence of the regime across most of the population. And there were other political organisations in Cuba whose supporters played an important role in the final days.

Had Castro acknowledged any of this, his undisputed authority would have been jeopardised – and much of that authority derived from the role that Che had played, particularly in the final period of struggle. So Fidel adopted apparently contradictory responses to Che. He was content to foster the myth of the tireless, irrepressible military leader, and to encourage a writing of the history of the struggle as a prolonged *military* campaign with Che as its symbol and its narrator. Yet he gave Che what was clearly a secondary role in the post-revolutionary political dispensation. For there was still a question mark over the degree of Che's agreement with Fidel's strategy, particularly concerning the exclusion of those forces with whom Che had found points of agreement and common action in the preceding months. There was one more consideration. Fidel was anxious not to do anything that might justify an immediate intervention by the US. Che had been outspoken in his anti-imperialism, while Fidel's caution was well known.[79]

Che agreed without demur. What does that tell us about him? First, that Che was loyal to a fault and accepted his own subordinate role as a foreigner fighting in Cuba. Second, as his writings show, Che saw military considerations as the priority. He was convinced that this was an armed victory first and foremost – and therefore saw discipline and a structure of command as the central organisational priority.

That is why he accepted Castro's announcement that Santiago would be the provisional capital of the new Cuba and stepped aside so that Camilo, the young leader brought up in Havana, should lead the victory parade and take the key military installation of Colombia while Che was sent to the less important Cabaña fort across Havana Bay. Che's unquestioning acceptance was a generous and selfless gesture.[80] Anderson agrees that Fidel wanted Che out of the limelight – although he offers the most generous explanation, to do with the international reception of the Cuban Revolution.[81]

When Che marched into La Cabaña early on 3 January, he addressed the soldiers who had just surrendered as 'neo-colonialist' troops and mocked, 'You can show us how to march but we'll show you how to fight.' The immediate task for Che was to prepare for the triumphant arrival of Fidel, and to organise 'revolutionary justice'. Meanwhile Castro was moving at speed to shape the new order. The presidency went to a moderate politician, Manuel Urrutia. It was a gesture towards foreign public opinion, but no more than a token. The rest of the cabinet was made up entirely of 26 July Movement nominees. The Directorio leadership, Che's very recent comrades in arms Chomón and Cubela, were furious. They moved into Havana and occupied the presidential palace, a significant act since their leader and best militants had died there in a failed assassination attempt on Batista just two years earlier. It was Che who went to speak with them and persuade them to move to a less high-profile building.

Fidel's convoy rolled into Havana on 9 January 1959. Camilo and Che were beside him on his jeep, though the best known of all the photographs of that day shows Camilo with Fidel, standing and engrossed in conversation. When Che does figure, he appears to be thoughtful and looking in a different direction. It might be that his mind was on the immediate task with which Castro had charged him – to dispense revolutionary justice in La Cabaña. Though it is not entirely clear how many were executed in those first days, it was probably about 55 (another 70 were summarily executed by Raúl in Oriente). By May the number had probably risen to around 550. These were the torturers, the police spies, the most zealous servants of Batista's police state.

In the excitement and din of the first revolutionary days in Havana, no one mourned their passing. In the streets, people were already exacting their own revenge, accompanied by singing and dancing and a kind of frenzy.[82] Che's puritanical streak had shown itself repeatedly in the course of the rebellion, and he was clearly shocked by the open sensuality and wildness of the city. At that time Havana symbolised a freedom and lack of inhibition that he, like many of his peasant soldiers, had never experienced. He was clearly concerned by its impact on his soldiers, and by their tendency to disappear into the bars and brothels of the port city. But previous experience had shown him that it was unwise to impose prohibitions on fighters who had so recently faced death. Instead he opted for a kind of mass marriage ceremony within the fortress, legitimising the uninhibited sexuality of the young soldiers.

The combination of a desire for retribution and the feeling of a carnival is not as contradictory as it might seem. Just as people celebrated their freedom, so they denounced those who had curtailed and compromised their liberty in earlier times. There was no question that those who were executed were for the most part people who had been guilty of terrible crimes against the population – it might even be argued that this was a way of restraining the more arbitrary and uncontrollable justice of the revolutionary crowd. And although the process was quick and ruthless, at least after the first day, it was conducted according to consistent rules of procedure, with an opportunity for defence.

In any event, Che would not shrink from a responsibility he had willingly taken on. He had personally shot deserters and argued for death sentences to be passed on informers in the mountains. In the framework of a political method whose first necessity was discipline and obedience, this was consistent. But the armed struggle was over now, and the consolidation of a new state raised different questions. While the policies for national development and independence were at least set out in embryo in earlier documents and statements, issues of democracy and liberty pressed in on the new Cuban leaders. They should have been priorities in the construction of a new society which, in Che's stated view – if not yet in Castro's – was set on a socialist path.

The suspension of the summary trials came soon enough, but in response to the pressure of public opinion abroad, particularly in the United States. From then on, the servants of the old regime were tried in a sports stadium in a framework of revolutionary law, and the responsibility passed out of Che's hands.

He had other pressures on him. On 9 January his parents arrived in Havana. Their delight at their son's elevation is obvious in their beaming photographs. But they had also to deal with his role in dispensing harsh justice, and his messianic fervour. They were presented to Che's lover Aleida. Later that month there would be a much less comfortable meeting when Hilda, Che's Peruvian wife, and their three year old daughter Hildita also arrived in Havana to discover Che's new domestic arrangements. Che was oddly reluctant to face this relatively less dangerous situation, and sent an aide to meet her and explain the situation!

By 12 January his asthma had become crippling and he left for a house by the sea at Tarará, where he remained, often virtually bedridden, for the next four months. He was just 15 miles outside Havana, but he was on the outer edges of public politics. Yet the situation was contradictory, for while he was clearly kept at arm's length from the construction of a political leadership, he was in many senses its political ideologue and one of its key symbolic representatives.[83]

There are three dimensions to these early days of revolution. First, the consolidation of the new power in the state. Second, the development of policies for a new government – because the truth is that very little in the way of strategic thinking had happened in the previous two years. Third, the impact of the Cuban Revolution on the rest of Latin America and the world in general.

Revolutionary Cuba was a small island of some eight million people. It still depended for almost the whole of its foreign earnings on sugar, exported in its entirety to the United States. It had little in the way of manufacturing capacity and most of its consumer goods, machinery, oil and energy requirements and tourist income came from the US. The relationship with Washington, therefore, was a determining factor in Cuba's past and in its future.

Che was adamant that the US remained the principal enemy, an imperialist power that could not behave in any other way. Castro shared that view, but was more inclined to seek out supporters and sympathisers in the United States who might constrain Washington's ability to act in a directly confrontational way. That was why Manuel Urrutia was the Cuban president and not (for a few months at least) Castro himself. Within a few months Castro would tour Latin America and go to the US to attempt to mobilise public opinion in Cuba's support. But by then things had moved on in Cuba itself.

Che was not in Tarará solely as a rest cure. He was involved in a series of discussions and preparations with leading figures in the new state. Their purpose was to create a new state security system, to develop economic policies, and to shape the relationship between Cuba and the rest of Latin America. Increasingly the discussions involved members of the PSP, who were beginning to establish their influence with Castro, with the encouragement of Che.

Cuban state security, G-2, was quickly organised and placed under the control of Ramiro Valdés, a trusted collaborator from Escambray.[84] Contacts with other Latin American revolutionaries were established, and many flew to Cuba to drink in the atmosphere of revolutionary fervour. Most urgent, perhaps, were the talks about Cuban economic policy, for it was soon clear to everyone that Washington was not for turning.

This was 1959, after all – still the era of the Cold War. The US had established itself as a global power and justified its political and military interventions across the world in terms of the conflict with the Soviet Union. Any bid for national self-determination or for autonomous development was represented as part of this confrontation – hence the US interventions in Lebanon, Iran, Guatemala and elsewhere. But despite its swaggering military presence, Washington's patronage of dictatorships across Latin America was a source of rage and resistance. A tour of Latin America by Nelson Rockefeller in 1958 had produced demonstrations and protests wherever he went.

Against this background, the Cuban Revolution and the overthrow of Batista was received with the same unrestrained joy throughout Latin America as it was in the streets of Havana. Batista was a stereotypical military ruler in many ways – most Latin American countries had their own recognisable variant of the model, each held in place and supported by the US. After a decade in which the North Americans had deployed their military and economic power with arrogant certainty, Cuba announced that the giant had feet of clay. The monstrous empire *could* be confronted, and its favoured representatives overthrown. That was the message that coursed through a generation of anti-imperialists.

In the US, too, Cuba sparked a public debate about America's role in the world. C Wright Mills, a sociologist and opponent of American power, produced his own warning to the US government[85] that nations denied their freedom would fight for it. Others, like Scheer and Zeitlin,[86] offered a similar warning from a very different political perspective. They argued that the legitimate demands for development and progress were not intrinsically Communist, but that if these basic human aspirations were denied then liberation movements would move to the left and become Communist. These voices were ignored, of course. US President Eisenhower was a Cold Warrior – and his notorious vice-president Richard Nixon even more so.

The powerful interests, military and economic, that controlled the US government understood the lessons well – but their response was to use every means at their disposal to undermine and destroy the new Cuban regime. There may, briefly, have seemed to be some hesitation on their part, but already the CIA and State Department agencies were denouncing this new government for its dedication to purposes more far-reaching than political independence. And at the centre of their interpretations was the figure of Che Guevara who, from their point of view, was more evidently a Communist than the wily Castro. Che may have withdrawn to convalesce, but their view was that he remained a central political force. And they may have been right.

At Tararé some of the people who Che had gathered around him in Escambray now came together again to discuss policy. And Latin Americans came to discuss the making of the revolution in their countries. It was, of course, not just one more political discussion over rum and cigars. They had come to speak to the man who had made a revolution – and what he said carried with it the enormous authority and weight of a successful revolutionary. There was no question of debate here – they had come to learn.

In those first months of 1959 Castro was forging the structures of his new state while Che was shaping its ideology and writing its history. In doing that, with the stature he possessed, he was not only describing recent experience – he was advocating that experience as a model and a method to be followed. Taken together, *Guerrilla Warfare* and his *Reminiscences of the Cuban Revolutionary War* comprised a political handbook as well as a military one. Their influence would be obvious in every major revolutionary struggle in Latin America for the next ten years or more. The consequences would, for the most part, be catastrophic.

Che's interpretation of the Cuban experience reflected and reinforced Castro's political vision. Che begins his Guerrilla Warfare, written in 1960, with a famous statement that the Cuban Revolution 'showed plainly the capacity of the people to free themselves by means of guerrilla warfare from a government that oppresses them'. He goes on to draw 'three fundamental lessons' from the Cuban Revolution:

(1) Popular forces can win a war against an army.
(2) It is not always necessary to wait until all conditions for making revolution exist: the insurrection can create them.
(3) In underdeveloped America, the countryside is the basic area for armed fighting.[87]

In this theory, it is revolutionaries who make the revolution – and indeed who create the revolutionary situation. The key factors governing success or failure, in this view, are fighting skill, bravery, heroism.

Translated into the business of forging a new kind of state, this political method assumed that it would be brought into being and sustained by the will of the leaders – and that the relationship between state and society would be one of command. The nature of the guerrilla struggle, and its leadership by the 26 July Movement under Castro, also meant that no mass organisations or organs of workers' self-defence had grown in the course of the revolutionary war. That was a necessary consequence of a war conducted until its very final moments in areas remote from the centres of population and political culture. The collapse of the Movement's urban base after the failed general strike of 1958 removed one possibility of building outside the mountains. The domination of the trade union movement by the Communists excluded another arena in which forms of mass activity might have developed in conjunction with the armed actions, given the conflict that had always existed between Castro and the Communist Party (despite recent attempts at rapprochement). The very speed of Batista's collapse was another inhibiting factor.

The only force ready to assume power, therefore, was the rebel army itself. No doubt this was how Fidel intended it should be. But the crucial result was that mass democratic participation had no place in this ideology of revolutionary warfare.

It is important to underline how far away this was from the revolutionary socialist tradition, and how remote from the central tenets of Marxism as the theory and practice of *workers' revolution*. In Che's description of the revolutionary process there is a fundamental and glaring omission.

Where are the masses? Where is the working class, whose liberation is the very definition of socialism? Marx wrote:

> Revolution is necessary...not only because the ruling class cannot be overthrown in any other way, but also because only in a revolution can the class overthrowing it succeed in ridding itself of all the muck of ages and become fitted to found society anew.[88]

This notion that revolution comprises the *self-emancipation* of the working class is absolutely central to Marx's thought. From being the objects of the interests of others, the majority become the governors of their own lives by transforming society through their own actions. It is a core principle in revolutionary Marxism. Yet the guerrilla war theory replaces this idea with another – that the *revolutionaries* will make the revolution on behalf of the wider class.

However, this right to represent is entirely self-proclaimed, based only on dangerous and ephemeral measures – popularity and acclaim.[89] That is entirely different from a right to leadership won in day to day struggle, in political practice, and rooted in an organic and democratic link with the class on whose behalf the revolutionaries claim to be acting. The guerrilla theory makes a virtue of the *separation* between revolutionaries and workers.

In the context of 1959, however, these ideas were imbued with the enormous stature and authority of the Cuban Revolution and its most influential symbol – Guevara. In the days and weeks after the removal of Batista, the 26 July Movement took power throughout Cuba and created a culture of celebration of the guerrilla as the new popular hero.

Carlos Franqui, the journalist who had spent the last

year of the campaign with Fidel and edited the rebel newspaper, now transformed it into the main daily paper. Everywhere there appeared portraits of heroic bearded guerrillas, and the language of politics echoed the rhetoric of armed struggle. Franqui's book *La Sierra y el Llano* (*The Mountains and the Plain*) cemented the mythology of a movement divided between the true revolutionaries in the mountains and the compromisers and cowards in the cities – except for exceptions like Frank País. This interpretation of the revolution consolidated the domination of Castro and Che's section of the movement, and gave a clear signal to the rival factions, the Communists and the Directorio, as to how control would be exercised in the revolutionary state.

Che Guevara speaking to the Cuban Trade Union Federation (CTC) in 1962   Osvaldo Salas

10 | Spreading the revolution

In the discussions with Latin American revolutionaries, it was these values and this method that were commended – and who would argue with those who had just won a revolution? They flocked to Havana and to Che's seaside retreat.

Who were these young revolutionaries? Their background, in many cases, was not so very different from Che's or Castro's – they came largely from the middle class and were driven above all by a hatred of imperialism. They were largely nationalists for whom national independence and self-determination was the most important issue. For the most part they did not come from a Communist tradition. The Communist parties of Latin America were embedded in the trade unions and had long since abandoned a revolutionary strategy in favour of a more gradual approach to social change. When Che insisted that revolutionaries need not wait for the objective conditions for revolution to exist, he was obliquely referring to the Communist parties. To him, and his generation of young revolutionary nationalists, it seemed the Communists had abandoned any hope of radical change except at the most abstract rhetorical level.

For all these reasons, those who came to Cuba in search of a method and a strategy were sympathetic to Che's views. In June 1959 an expedition led by a Sierra Maestra veteran landed in the Dominican Republic with the intention of setting up a guerrilla unit. Within hours 230 people were dead, massacred by the soldiers of the dictator Trujillo.[90] A plan to realise a similar operation in Haiti a few weeks later was shelved. In November, in Paraguay, a group of 80 crossed the Argentine frontier with plans to create a guerrilla army to fight the Stroessner dictatorship there. Only ten people survived the volley of bullets which met them as they stepped into Paraguay. Earlier that year Roberto Romero, whom Che had met four years earlier, led what would be a disastrous expedition into Nicaragua.[91]

This was not all that Che was doing out of the public eye. A US intelligence report early in 1959 suggested that he was, in fact, the key political thinker behind the scenes. Certainly he had assembled around him a group of experts – some of whom had moved to Escambray during the Las Villas campaign – to look at issues of policy for the new regime. Some of them came from the Communist Party, which might explain the extreme secrecy of these meetings and discussions. Castro himself was concerned that if news of these secret gatherings got out the US would use them to justify an intervention against Cuba.

Yet there is no doubt Che was centrally involved in these first months in three major projects. The first was the transformation of the rebel army into a permanent force to defend the new state. That defence involved the creation of a security apparatus, which also fell under Che's aegis. The second area of discussion was economic, and above all involved the preparation of an agrarian reform bill based on the ideas that Che had argued for a year earlier. The third area concerned the political direction of the revolution. Here Che (and Raúl Castro) certainly believed that the 26 July Movement and the Communists should move closer to each other. Fidel was far more cautious, especially when it came to letting this be made public. His long-term suspicion of the PSP remained, although he had continued to meet and talk with Carlos Rafael Rodríguez, a leader of the PSP, throughout the previous year. In any event, the approaches were careful and delicate, though Che was in favour of more robust discussions.

In a sense, the political debates were more sharply addressed in other areas – particularly on the question of agrarian reform. In a single-product, agricultural economy, this was necessarily the central issue – because it addressed the questions of diversification, growth and modernisation at the same time.

Recent experience provided two models which might be followed. One would involve dismantling the large, particularly foreign-owned, estates and redistributing the land as small farms. This would create a class of peasant farmers whose holdings, to be viable, would be of a size that would allow them to employ some labour to work the land. The farmers would become, essentially, small capitalists with conservative attitudes towards a capitalist system of which they were obviously beneficiaries. After the Cuban Revolution the US began to advocate agrarian reform of this conservative kind through the Alliance for Progress – it was implemented, for example, in Chile in 1964, although largely unsuccessfully.

The alternative might be described as a revolutionary reform, in which the great estates would be 'collectivised' – run as collective social projects. The particular advantage of this kind of reorganisation is that it would provide an income from an agricultural surplus which the state, as the ultimate controller of the land, could use – to invest in industrial growth, for example. However, peasants have historically opposed this kind of reform because, in effect, it destroys the material basis for their existence.

Che clearly favoured the second alternative. When the first revolutionary law was passed in the Escambray mountains in 1958 there had already been an argument which Che clearly did not win. The issue arose again now. What was the purpose of land reform? Was it to take the large estates and farms, both foreign and Cuban-owned, and redistribute them among the small peasant farmers, giving each a small farm? Or should the purpose be to transform those holdings into co-operatives and collective farms which could be adapted to produce something other than sugar?

Beyond this lay the bigger question that Guevara, more than anyone else in the leadership, believed was the key to the future of the revolution. How could a small economy, dependent for more than 80 percent of its export earnings on one product – sugar – break its dependency? One answer was to diversify the economy – the other was to develop industrially.

There was a further component of this strategic vision – an international environment which was more open to and sympathetic with the revolution. All these things were intimately connected.[92] As a result, Che clearly saw himself as involved in building a socialist society in Cuba and spreading the revolution beyond the island.

He believed a breakthrough would be achieved beyond Cuba by the export of the guerrilla war. It was, after all, the only political experience Guevara could refer to – he had neither knowledge nor a political understanding of how the mass of working people could make a revolution for themselves. Significantly, Che described the new army as 'the vanguard of the Cuban people'.[93] This was a clear declaration that the army would play the key political role ascribed in the revolutionary socialist tradition to a revolutionary party embedded in the collective organisations of workers. But Che saw mass working-class organisation as something that would *follow* a seizure of power and be brought into being by the new state.

The first Law of Agrarian Reform was passed on 7 May. It echoed very closely a speech Che had made on the issue a month earlier. The redistribution of land to small farmers and landless agricultural workers began later that month. In January 1960 the government announced the nationalisation of all the *latifundia* (the large, privately-owned estates), whether Cuban or foreign-owned. More important, Fidel announced they would be transformed into collective farms or co-operatives rather than small private farms. This was the kind of agrarian reform that Che had argued for in the Escambray mountains and which Fidel had resisted then. It would be seen as a gauntlet thrown down to the US and its friends in Cuba.

Why was this so significant? The creation of a new class of small individual farmers would signal that Cuba was moving towards a modern, capitalist system in which the means of production were privately owned. The turn towards co-operatives and collective farms was embedded in an idea of *social property* – that the resources of society belonged to all and should be used for the benefit of all. In fact, the state now became the proprietor of the land.

The nationalisation a month earlier of the US-owned telephone and electricity companies had already been interpreted by sectors of US intelligence as proof that the regime was Communist. And it was Che whom they saw as responsible. This went a long way to explaining why Castro had such a frosty reception when he travelled to Washington that same month. President Eisenhower evaded the meeting by going on a golf trip, leaving his vice-president Richard Nixon, a virulent anti-Communist, to deal with Fidel. Nixon's report on the meeting concluded that Cuba was Communist and should be dealt with quickly. Fidel, on the other hand, went out of his way throughout his tour to present himself as a nationalist, and that the new Cuba did not represent a danger to its old master.

From the US, Castro flew on to Brazil and Venezuela for a diplomatic love-in with the presidents of those countries whom he clearly saw (wrongly as it turned out) as potential allies. In a well documented stopover in Houston, Fidel met Che and Raúl. There is no record of their conversations, but it may well be the two radicals were concerned that Fidel had bent too far in his approaches to the US government. He had announced unilaterally that there would be no more executions, for example, despite the fact that there were several unfinished trials. Raúl and Che completely opposed what they saw as this sop to US public opinion.

On 2 June 1959 Che married Aleida at the house of one of his closest friends and associates, Alberto Castellanos.[94] It was 12 days before his 31st birthday.

The announcement, three days after his wedding, that Che was to be sent on a diplomatic mission to several countries – he would be away for three months – raised some eyebrows:

> Was this part of Fidel's usual game of checks and balances? Was Che angry at the moderation of the revolutionary process as some of the people who knew him suggest?[95]

On the one hand, it fitted perfectly with the search for allies and economic partners across the world. On the other, it removed for a while the man whose political authority had grown so dramatically that it could rightly be seen to challenge Fidel's own. It might also be seen as a gesture to Washington, where the atmosphere was becoming more hostile by the day to the new Cuban state.

Che's journey began on 12 June. Aleida did not go with him, despite the urgings of his friends to 'take the chance and make it a honeymoon'. Che's decision to go alone was one more example of his austerity, his anxiousness not to appear to have any other purpose than to further the revolution. There was no doubt that the Cuban people noticed, and were impressed. For Che, the tour was a contradictory experience, sometimes frustrating, sometimes exhilarating, as he travelled to Egypt, Indonesia, Japan and Yugoslavia. But his letters return again and again to themes of loneliness and the 'sense of mission' that drove him.

Guevara had become a man with a sense of historical destiny, of his importance on the world stage.[96] Yet he was never described by those who met him as arrogant – impatient with protocol, restless, demanding yes, but never aloof. The covert negotiations with the Soviet Union for the purchase of Cuban sugar were perhaps the most important element of the trip. Given the increasingly shrill accusations coming out of the US these were kept very quiet. So too was the arrival early in October of the first official Soviet representative to Cuba. Was this a sign that Fidel was moving left? It is hard to know whether it was one more balancing act by Castro – looking for new markets while not offering any wider commitment.

When Che returned, the Agrarian Reform Institute (INRA) was functioning under the direction of Fidel. A new responsibility – as head of its industrial department – awaited him. Politically, it coincided with other developments, all of which consolidated Castro's control of the state.

The new appointment was, in one sense, entirely logical – Che had always argued it was necessary to develop an industrial base as quickly as possible. He believed it was a condition of survival. Cuban factories were suffering badly from the lack of spare parts and the effective closure of their external markets. There was little investment, as the gradual leakage of Cuba's employer class was already beginning. Enticed by the US, for whom their flight was an important propaganda weapon, and threatened by the encroachment of the state on the economy, the old business and professional classes began to organise their departure. It was symbolic that when Che took over his department the building was unfinished, the offices empty, the equipment negligible. Yet Che once again appeared as Fidel's second in command.

There were developments elsewhere too. In July President Urrutia and his allies resigned from government in protest at the leftward direction of government policy. After a sham refusal, Fidel allowed himself to be appointed president by acclaim as he 'yielded' to the people's will at a Havana rally commemorating 26 July. More seriously, Huber Matos – an old comrade, an important guerrilla commander and one of those Che had described as the 'old anti-Communists' – also announced his resignation. Fidel insisted that he be tried for treason, and the leaders of the revolution argued over whether or not he should be executed. Raúl insisted that *any* opposition to the government in the current climate was treason and should be punished accordingly. Others held their ground and argued that dissent was not treason. Che seems to have vacillated, though in the end he moved from advocating execution to accepting the 30-year jail sentence eventually imposed on Matos.

As if he did not have enough to do already, in late

November Guevara was named president of the Cuban National Bank. This was first and foremost a political appointment – the previous directors clearly favoured business and were hostile to Fidel. Further, the bank may well have been complicit in the haemorrhage of people and resources to Miami, as the exiles sailed away in numbers across the 90-mile Florida Straits.

There is an apocryphal story that describes Fidel asking if there were any economists in the room and Che putting up his hand – he claimed later that he had misheard, thinking Fidel had asked for 'Communists'. The reality is that Fidel had very little choice. The group of trusted allies in the leadership of the new state were very few. Camilo was dead and Raúl was now in charge of the defence ministry. Che was no economist, though he was reading and studying both economics and mathematics. But he could be absolutely relied on to establish political control over the economy through the bank. That was his real task. And it represented a clear move in the direction of a centralised, planned economy, even if this was not yet explicit. When it was, Che would find himself in disagreement over how a socialist economy should be organised. But that came later.

The stockmarket in New York shuddered at the news of Che's appointment, and several more investors began to pull their money out of Cuba. They saw a new direction in Cuban policy, alhough it was neither as systematic nor as organised as they imagined. By the end of the first year of revolution, the remnants of the old regime had been largely swept out of the army, the police, the economic institutions and the organs of government. Fidel headed the state and the Agrarian Reform Institute, Che controlled the security apparatus and the National Bank, and Raúl commanded the army. The US was adopting a hard line towards Cuba, combining a mounting economic siege with the creation of regional security arrangements to isolate the country. It was moving quickly to neutralise the political echoes of the Cuban Revolution in Latin America. The documents circulating in US government circles pointed again and again to Che's central role as evidence of the direction the process was taking.

The visit of a Soviet vice-president, Mikoyan, to Cuba in February 1960 was a catalyst. He was there ostensibly to open a Soviet industrial exhibition, but there were other agendas at work. Given the unofficial embargo already in place, the Russians were seen as a potential market for Cuban sugar and supplier of consumer goods. The relationship was not just financial, it was political. Che's team of economic advisers came from all over Latin America, and they were Communists to a person. That meant they shared a view of economic development based on the concept of planning practised in the Communist bloc. They recommended using the income from sugar sales to fund industrial development, to divert funds from consumption into production. This would be carried through in a highly centralised way, using strict criteria of profitability. Che's first measure, however, was more directly political – he restricted the currency reserves. This was an obvious prelude to bringing all foreign trade under the bank's control, although that would not be decreed for another year.

The reaction of Washington was entirely predictable. The United States's most important weapon was the dependence of Cuba on the US to buy its sugar – its major source of foreign currency. Washington now threatened to cut the sugar quota (the amount it undertook to buy) in the light of the nationalisation of the big estates. It also began to arm the small groups of Cuban exiles who were preparing to invade.

In March 1960 Che demanded that the US-owned oil refineries process the shipments of Russian oil that were beginning to arrive. When the corporations refused, the Cuban government expropriated the installations. There was very little choice since Cuba had no oil reserves of its own. The oil shipments were part of a commercial agreement signed a month earlier with the Soviet Union, which among other things guaranteed the purchase of significant quantities of Cuban sugar. At the same time, and this would turn out to be critically important later, Cuba set up a joint national economic council, JUCEPLAN, under the powerful influence of Soviet advisers. The council represented a clear decision to move towards the Soviet model of a centralised, planned economy.

Assaults and raids from bases in the US were becoming more frequent, and Castro was convinced that the defence of the island was an urgent priority. Arms-purchasing trips were proving fruitless, however. For example, Britain was uncharacteristically reluctant to sell arms to this potential new customer. Obviously Washington was twisting arms and only Belgium and Italy seemed willing to supply Cuba with weapons. The need for a defence strategy became more pressing when the first shipload of Belgian arms exploded in Havana harbour, killing 100 people. It was certainly sabotage. So in May 1960 Cuba and the Soviet Union concluded an arms agreement.

The pace of events was intensifying. Havana had changed:

The city that a year before had still been an American playground of exclusive yacht clubs, private beaches, casinos and brothels – and whites-only neighbourhoods – was disappearing. The roulette wheels were still spinning in the big hotels, but most of the prostitutes were off the streets.[97]

Relations with the United States were close to breaking point. The people around Eisenhower, like Richard Nixon and the CIA, were more and more openly advocating direct action against a Cuba they now saw as an outpost of the Soviet bloc. Anti-Castro fighters were actively recruited in the US, particularly in Miami where a long-established Cuban population was swollen by the addition of a growing number of exiles, almost entirely professionals and businessmen, as well as servants of the old regime and those who had represented US interests on the island.

In July the threat to cut Cuba's sugar quota materialised in a vote by the US Congress. The Cuban government responded with further nationalisations of US-owned properties. At the same time there were guerrillas once again in the mountains of Escambray, including some of Che's old comrades. Yet they were fighting the revolution. The rebellion was short-lived – within weeks they were caught and executed – but the stakes were getting higher. The political opposition and its newspapers were largely suppressed by the middle of 1960. In the US Cuba began to take an increasingly central role in the developing presidential campaign in which John F Kennedy ridiculed rival candidate Richard Nixon for his failure to act against Cuba and promised that he would take decisive action as soon as he occupied the White House.

This war of words and exchange of accusations often veiled the real interests at the heart of the argument. The US government faced a challenge to its domination and its hitherto uncontested right to control world affairs with its combination of economic and military power. Cuban sugar was really neither here nor there, but Cuban defiance was intolerable.[98]

Inside Cuba there was a real political transformation going on, and Che was increasingly at its centre. In the trade unions, for example, a battle had been under way for over a year. After the revolution the CTC, the Cuban workers' congress, had fallen under the control of a group of members of the 26 July Movement around David Salvador. Like many of his generation, he was bitterly hostile to the Cuban Communists. By the end of 1959, however, Castro himself was growing increasingly anxious about the group's influence, which he saw as essentially conservative. By the year's end, Salvador had been replaced by a new leadership closely allied to the Communist Party. By mid-1960 the trade unions were organised from above, directly by the minister of labour. They had become an arm of the state.

Che Guevara on a voluntary working day helping to build the Alamar housing complex on the outskirts of Havana, 1961

Osvaldo Salas

11 | **The measures taken**

On 10 July 1960 Fidel was unwell and Che took his place at a rally with Khrushchev, the Soviet leader. Che's speech was triumphant and confident. The revolutionary state, he said, now enjoyed the protection of the second most powerful military state in the world. It is not really so surprising that he should say this. Even before the revolution he had increasingly described himself as a Communist in the Soviet mould, and a majority of those around him – before and after the overthrow of Batista – were Communists.

But it is very clear that Che's interpretation of what it meant to be a Communist was very different from Marx's classic formulation of a socialist revolution as the moment when the working class takes power for itself. His book *Guerrilla Warfare*, published in April 1960, was emphatic that the protagonists of revolution were the revolutionaries, who stood above the majority and acted on their behalf. Once in power, it was the revolutionary state that assumed this role. The key to success was economic growth and diversification, and clarity of command. The revolutionary state was simply another manifestation of the guerrilla army.

What was missing in this picture was democracy, control from below and a leadership accountable directly to the majority it claimed to speak for. However, this was not an issue for Che or for Fidel, who on May Day had coined a new slogan, 'Yes to the revolution, no to elections'.

For Che, the key issues were 'sacrifice and dedication'.[99] The tensions with the United States were deepening by the day, and any thought of negotiations which Fidel might once have entertained were now forgotten. Che had always emphasised his implacable hostility to imperialism, and his conviction that it would never allow the revolution to progress. Washington was already covertly supporting armed resistance to the new regime and was determined to use its economic power to undermine revolutionary Cuba. Against this, Che's writings and speeches at the time obstinately emphasise turning to the Soviet Union both for support and supplies (for oil, in particular) and as a market for Cuban sugar.

At this stage, Che also saw the Soviet economy as a model to be followed, since it had undertaken the rapid collectivisation of agriculture followed by equally rapid industrialisation. We know now that growth was achieved at the expense of millions of Russian workers, and by the imposition of a command economy in which the state organised the exploitation of labour under conditions of terror.[100] But it is probable that Che was unaware of this terrible history – despite the 1956 speech by Khrushchev which had begun to tear away the mask of Stalin's rule. Che's most urgent concern was industrial development which could reduce Cuba's dependence on sugar by developing other areas of the economy, and stimulate the production of the raw materials and machinery needed to sustain that production.

The anniversary of the 1953 assault on the Moncada barracks, 26 July, is often the occasion for the announcement of key changes of direction in Cuba. In 1960 the tone and content of Fidel Castro's invariably long speech was combative and challenging. For the first time, Fidel sent out a warning to the rest of Latin America that wherever there was injustice and oppression, the Cuban example would serve to inspire resistance and a revolutionary struggle. The speech was, of course, as much for US consumption as for Latin America's. It did signal a hardening line towards the imperialists, but it was also a sign of things to come in Cuba itself.

Most of all, it was the clearest indication of Che's political and personal influence on the revolution. This was expressed in several ways: first, in a hardening anti-imperialism; second, in the developing relationship with the Soviet Union and with the Cuban Communists; third, in an economic policy which increasingly emphasised a swift diversification away from sugar; and fourth, in internal policies within the Cuban state which increasingly emphasised the military elements of discipline, sacrifice and obedience.

When Castro visited New York to address the United Nations in June, his attitude was very different from a year earlier. His three-hour speech was the longest on record (though not his longest by a very long way) and threw down a gauntlet to Washington. In New York the delegation won a huge public relations victory by refusing the suite set aside in the Waldorf Astoria (which was too expensive and almost certainly bugged) and moving to a guesthouse in Harlem. If that made the Cubans very popular among working-class people, it won them no new friends in the US administration. On the other hand, both candidates in the coming presidential election (Nixon and

Kennedy) had already made clear their determination to 'do something about Cuba'.

Within Cuba there were clear signs of a tightening of state control. The creation of what would become the Committees for the Defence of the Revolution (CDRs) at the end of September sent out a very clear message. On the surface they were a response to an intensification of internal resistance, sabotage and the increase in number of armed opposition groups. But at the same time they were a visible and organised form of direct state control. Indeed, like most of the other organisations created under the leadership of the 26 July Movement, they were characteristically a means to ensure that decisions made by the government were carried through. There was no sense at all that the communication could function in reverse, no sense that these committees could represent the grassroots of society before their leaders. The same changes had occurred in the trade union movement, for example, where the new union congress (CTC) spoke on behalf of government to the workers rather than the other way around. The Federation of Cuban Women (FMC) functioned in much the same way. All were instruments of the state.

In the tense atmosphere of those times – with the arrival of the first Russian arms shipments, the detention of armed insurgents, the virtual severing of economic and political relations with Washington coupled with mounting and increasingly overt threats – the argument that this was an emergency in which normal rules did not apply probably carried a great deal of weight with ordinary people. Yet the long-term consequence was an acceptance of, or at least a resignation to, the idea that democracy and transparency were luxuries that a revolution under siege could not afford. More than 40 years later, it is an argument still used by the Cuban government and by its supporters abroad.

It was Che who argued that allegiance to the revolution was the primary issue, and that failure to adhere to its demands was an offence and should be punished. It was Che who created the extremely controversial labour camp at Guanacahabibes where 'those who had committed crimes against revolutionary morals' were sent to be rehabilitated through hard labour.[101]

Opposition presses were shut down, and pre-revolutionary magazines and newspapers closed. The enforced shutdown of the cultural supplement *Lunes de Revolución* earlier in the year, for example, came as the direct result of the short film called *PM* made by some of the people involved with *Lunes* which showed a decadent and hedonistic Havana life. It could not be characterised as counter-revolutionary in any sense – unless, of course, homosexuality was regarded as such in and of itself! It was an early sign of the persecution of gays, always identified by Castro with a decadent pre-1959 Havana, which would continue throughout the following four decades.[102]

In Latin America the Cuban Revolution still enjoyed an enormous authority when it came to organising the struggle – guerrilla war was the model now followed by a new generation. Che argued that revolutionaries conquered power first, and *then* made the revolution. The state commanded, and the rank and file carried through those instructions.

At the same time, Che now used a concept that would become central in his later thinking, the notion of the 'new man' (*el hombre nuevo*). It was already set out in his June 1960 speech 'On Sacrifice and Dedication', in which he argued that workers must accept material sacrifices in the present in exchange for a future in which their living standards would rise. Che argued then, and would argue more forcefully later, that concern with material benefits was one manifestation of a capitalist culture, and that in a new society service to the community and a sense of contributing to the revolution would be rewards enough in themselves. This would express itself particularly in voluntary labour days, when people gave their time for free. As time went on, this voluntary labour would gradually become an enforced extension of the working day without wages, and provoke growing if subterranean discontent.

It was a tantalising argument, except that the promises offered were offered more in hope than in certainty. In the meantime, for most workers it seemed that they were being asked to sacrifice their own interests in favour of a remote and unreliable future. In any event, the reality was that Cuba was in no position to determine its own economic future, especially when it was dependent on a much more powerful economic interest (that of Russia) which controlled its resources and the price of its goods. In that respect the situation was not so very different from the period before 1959, when Cuba had depended on the US to buy its sugar and sell it the consumer goods it needed. The revolution did not mean those goods of which the majority of people had been deprived for so long would now become available. On the contrary, it would mean they were even less available than before.

But there were important benefits. The literacy campaign of 1960 brought literacy levels to the highest in Latin America,[103] and health provision in those first years won Cuba a justified reputation for basic healthcare. These were undeniable social advances that benefited everyone. But there was very soon a problem. The accumulation of wealth to finance production and new areas in the economy would redirect resources away from social provision. Che's concept of a new consciousness was an answer to that problem.

At first, the response of the Cuban population was extremely positive. Yet there was a missing element in Che's argument. Involvement and participation could be ends in themselves, provided they were real. Endless declarations of loyalty by the leaders to the led, however, were no substitute for a genuine workers' democracy in which it was the popular organisations which made the decisions and the government which carried them out.

As these changes were taking place, Che was sent by Fidel on an official visit to Moscow. His visit coincided with a crucial meeting of the world's Communist parties – a meeting which would bring to the surface the mounting tension between the two Communist superpowers of the time, China and the Soviet Union. Che was received with acclaim. He stood beside the Soviet leader Khrushchev at the march past marking the anniversary of the Russian Revolution and was given access to the inner sanctums of the Soviet bureaucracy. Yet for all the embraces and the privileges, Che seems to have been completely unaware of what was actually happening during the Congress of Communist Parties:[104]

> Despite his Marxist sympathies, Guevara was unaware of the secret life of the Communist family. His understanding of the USSR was almost poetic. He had read a number of uplifting works by the writers that Stalin had described as the 'engineers of the soul', and watched the equally edifying films that extolled the virtues of 'positive heroes'… He took at face value everything he was shown or told or promised.[105]

From Che's point of view, the visit was a great success. He was received with full ceremony and placed at the right hand of what he called 'the second most powerful nation on earth'. The Eastern Europe he saw, of course, was the one he wanted to see. Che had no real experience of political life or the socialist movement. His avid reading of the previous two years was haphazard and largely concerned with technical matters and philosophy. In a word, he was naive.

The odd thing is that his innocence was in some sense part of his attraction – especially when it was combined with his incorruptibility and his extraordinary capacity for work. Yet it meant that he could be misled as to Russian intentions. And when he took a ten-day trip to China and Korea, he could say on his return that he saw no poverty in China, despite the terrible ravages wreaked by China's Great Leap Forward – its attempt to jump from economic backwardness into industrial modernity in a few short years. Similarly, he saw nothing in Russia or elsewhere in Eastern Europe to concern him.[106]

Che's views were unaffected by his visit. Indeed, it fuelled the optimism he expressed in his first television interview broadcast shortly after his return.[107] Cuban attitudes in 1961 were certainly reinforced by the conviction that the Soviets would defend them whatever the cost. In fact the main immediate concern of the Russians was to keep Cuba outside the sphere of Chinese influence. Yet although Che was hugely impressed by the Communist world, it did concern him that Soviet products were so shoddy compared with the North American goods that Cubans were used to. He addressed these issues in his TV broadcast. At the same time, he was impressed by China – and particularly, perhaps, by the ideas of the Great Leap Forward.

On 17 April 1961 an invasion force of 1,500 landed on the beach known as Playa Girón or the Bay of Pigs, on Cuba's southern coast. Officially denied by the US government, it had clearly been given the go-ahead by the new Kennedy administration and organised through the CIA.[108] Tension had been mounting for weeks before as the island was infiltrated by various groups and acts of sabotage grew more frequent. Despite a massive police round-up of 35,000 people in Havana and almost three times that number nationwide, some of whom were summarily executed, a major department store in Havana was blown up a week before the invasion. On 15 April two planes camouflaged to look like Cuban Air Force planes bombed Santiago and Havana, where seven were killed.[109] In his angry speech at the funeral the following day, Castro openly described the revolution as 'socialist' for the first time.

The armed invasion was a disaster. The Cuban militia reacted with speed and courage, and eight light planes dealt with the powerful but cumbersome B-26 bombers. In three days it was over, and Castro and Che were able to claim 'the first defeat of imperialism in the Americas'.[110] For Kennedy, in the atmosphere of Cold War confrontation, Cuba was simply a Soviet surrogate – and this was a battle lost to the imperial rival. The Soviets were cheerfully ready to let it be seen in that light. In May Fidel was awarded the Lenin Peace Prize, the Soviet equivalent of a Nobel Prize.

Kennedy's reaction was to raise the level of military spending. Che's analysis of Playa Girón was to see it as a confirmation of the guerrilla war strategy – Kennedy's was oddly similar. Where Che called for the building of guerrilla armies, Kennedy ordered the rapid development of counter-revolutionary forces and strategies. One product of the time was the first 'rapid deployment force', the Green Berets. The meeting of the Organisation of American States at Punta del Este, Uruguay, in August was ostensibly concerned with economic matters. But the undercurrents were tangible. The new aid programme was one more component of a counter-revolutionary strategy, offering routes to development other than (and opposed to) revolution.

Guevara was Cuba's representative at the conference, much to the delight of the photographers who presumably had been expecting to take pictures of grey suits for a week. In his speech on 8 August Che attacked the US, and called for economic justice and independence for the countries of Latin America. In reality the aggressiveness of his attack was tempered slightly by his declaration, later in the speech, that Cuba wanted to coexist with the 'American family as a whole'. Some time later he met in private with the US delegate Richard Goodwin. The records of that meeting did not surface for several decades – but they show Che was quite open about Cuba's economic problems and suggested a kind of 'standoff' to allow Cuba to concentrate on its immediate problems. In exchange, Che hinted that Cuba would no longer supply the armed struggle in Latin America or form formal alliances with the Soviets.

Goodwin's reports to his superiors show he interpreted the conversation as a sign of weakness. What of Che? The likelihood is that he saw Cuba as speaking from a position of momentary strength in the wake of Playa Girón. Kennedy, as was to be expected, saw it as an opportunity to escalate the pressure on Cuba, which was now going through serious economic difficulties, and pressed successive Latin American governments to break all ties with Cuba. The giant was flexing its muscles.

It seemed ironic now to reflect on Che's affirmation that by 1962 Cuba would be on its way to a programme of industrialisation and economic change, the reward for the sacrifice and selflessness of the Cuban people in postponing the material improvement of their lives and fighting in defence of the revolution. The military campaign against Cuba continued and the economic crisis deepened. By March 1962 ration cards appeared in Cuba:

> Although neither Che nor Fidel would acknowledge the fact, the advent of food rationing heralded the end of their illusion of making Cuba a self-sufficient socialist state, free of external dependencies. As for Che's illusion that a global fraternity of socialist nations could bring about the demise of capitalism, it was about to be dashed to pieces.[111]

Che took over the new Ministry of Industry in February 1962. Rationing began a month later. It was typical of Che, and an explanation for his abiding popularity, that he refused an additional ministerial allowance and insisted that he and everyone in his department must receive only their proper allocation. At the same time there was a new urgency in his speeches and writings, and a mounting sense of frustration. The US embargo was biting. Spare parts for the entirely US machinery that ran Cuban industry were running short and impossible to replace, although the Cubans were already developing the capacity for improvisation for which they have since become famous. Despite his appeals to the population to exercise restraint, money was still being spent on consumer goods, though these were growing scarce.

There was also a human problem. By now, 500,000 Cubans had fled to the US. These *gusanos* (worms), as they were called, really represented most of Cuban business and the bulk of her professionals – lawyers, doctors, technicians, engineers. Che reported that he had only two geologists in his department when he needed 2,000. Two hundred or so East European volunteers were far from sufficient to make up the numbers.[112] Even had they been willing to do so, the Soviet bloc could not provide sufficient spare parts or new machinery in the short or even the medium term, and what was available was largely of mediocre quality.[113] Then there was the acute shortage of raw materials.

For Che, the necessity of escape from dependency on sugar and for economic diversification was increasingly urgent. Yet between 1961 and 1963 sugar production fell, partly because of external conditions and partly because many of the new beneficiaries of land reform had once cut the cane, and now refused to do it. Che was coming face to face with the limitations on development in a single country – and with the contradictions of the Soviet model.

In his office on the ninth floor of the INRA (Agrarian Reform Institute) building in Revolution Square, Che displayed both his most positive and his more negative qualities. He was absolutely committed to the revolution, and willing to work for it to the exclusion of his personal life (as his wife Aleida knew only too well). But he also carried into everything the model of command that he had developed in the rebel army. As a result he created a huge and highly centralised bureaucracy with himself at its centre. He complained that the new state operated in a haphazard and improvised way, creative but disorganised and anarchic. His solution was to bring everything under the control of his ministry with himself as the ultimate authority. He was encouraged in this by his advisers, many of whom were Communists from elsewhere in Latin America.

By late 1961 the problems faced by a revolution under siege had still not been solved, and the bureaucratic system was still plagued by the difficulties and shortcomings Che had complained about. He clearly experienced a deepening sense of frustration, and irritation with his all too casual Cuban comrades. If the Bay of Pigs had produced political optimism in Che and Fidel, the material reality gave growing cause for concern. Che's response was to intensify his calls for sacrifice and dedication, his emphasis on self-denial. It was as if even the material conditions could be overcome by a massive effort of will, as if consciousness were an adequate substitute for the absent material resources. He clearly did not know, or perhaps did not acknowledge, the devastating social and human costs of rapid development in Russia and China – not to mention the vast natural resources available to both which Cuba lacked.

Che's impatience with material realities was at the heart of his political theory. If the revolutionaries could substitute for the masses in making the revolution, the revolutionary state could overcome the material limitations it faced, he argued. But part of that process of overcoming, for Che, also involved changing the political environment in which Cuba had to exist. If Washington was seeking every means to isolate the revolution politically and economically, then the revolution must counter that offensive with one of its own. By early 1962 Che was once again actively encouraging the construction of guerrilla movements across Latin America.

Within Cuba itself, Che was expressing some scepticism about the creeping domination of the Cuban Communists and the alliance with the 26 July Movement expressed in the new political organisation created the year before – the Integrated Revolutionary Organisation (ORI). But he enthusiastically supported the campaign against the Communist leader Escalante, and his subsequent exile. Che saw him as corrupt, self-seeking and undoubtedly as conspiring against the revolution.

Che Guevara, 1963   Osvaldo Salas

12 | **The 13 days and after**

Thirteen days in October changed many things, including the direction of the Cuban Revolution.[114] In the second half of 1962 the Soviet Union deployed arms and troops in Cuba – the final agreement was drawn up between Khrushchev, the Soviet leader, and Che in September. Of the 40 missiles based on the island, half had nuclear warheads or nuclear tips. There were also 42,000 Russian troops on the island.[115]

The most bizarre thing is that the US intelligence services seemed to be unaware of the build-up – at least until 16 October, when Kennedy was shown photographs taken by U-2 spy planes which showed launching pads under construction. Some of the president's advisers, whose attitudes towards Cuba were already well known, advised an immediate invasion. Kennedy opted instead for a naval blockade, preventing any Soviet ships from entering Cuban territorial waters. The Russian ships carrying weapons continued to sail towards Cuba. They would reach the blockade on the morning of 24 October – unless they turned back first.

Everyone who lived through those days remembers the tension and the fear as the deadline approached. For a decade the world had lived under the permanent threat of nuclear war between the US and the Soviet Union. The fact that the West possessed a nuclear capacity many times greater than the Russians meant nothing. Both had enough to destroy the world. The clock ticked closer and closer to the apocalyptic midnight as the Russian fleet held its course.[116] At around midday on 24 October, the Russians turned around – and the clock stopped.

Just a few days earlier Khrushchev and the Cuban government had vehemently denied that the missiles existed. Then, overnight, the Russian leader changed his position, acknowledged their existence, and negotiated a deal with the US government. The Russian missiles would be withdrawn if the US closed its Turkish bases and Washington undertook not to invade Cuba. Kennedy ignored the first part of the agreement, but both claimed a diplomatic victory.

Where were the Cubans in all this? It seemed very much as though Russia and the United States had played out this whole scenario with barely a nod in the direction of the Cuban government. Was Cuba ever anything more than a pawn in a bigger international game?

Che Guevara had no doubt when he met Khrushchev in September that the Soviets were sincere in their commitment to defend Cuba, though he was disconcerted by their refusal to make the military agreement public. Yet 'Che did not even imagine that Khrushchev might withdraw the missiles in the event of a confrontation with Washington',[117] and nor did Castro. On the contrary, they both believed the Russians would go to the wall in defence of Cuba out of political conviction. This was naive at best. Khrushchev certainly did want to prevent a US invasion of Cuba. At the same time, it is unlikely he was ready to risk global nuclear warfare to prevent this. It might have been a dangerous bargaining game on his part, or a way of testing US military intelligence and defences. But he will have known that the US surpassed Russia's nuclear capacity many times over.

Cuban claims that the missiles were imposed on Cuba by the Russians are questionable. Che and Castro had been negotiating arms deals with the Russians for some time, and both had already made reference to the missiles. Che certainly believed, and had repeated many times, his conviction that the 'socialist world' would defend Cuba whatever the cost.

For them, therefore, the agreement by the Russians to withdraw the missiles was a simple betrayal. Kennedy's agreement not to invade paled into insignificance beside the knowledge that when the crunch came Cuba was alone and isolated. While he said very little in public, Castro was enraged by what he saw as Russian cynicism. But he was a pragmatist and knew that Cuba still needed Russian economic and diplomatic support.

Within Cuba the impact of the crisis, though often beneath the surface, was profound. The growing influence of the Cuban Communists within the Castro government was always based to some extent on the Soviet connection. The Escalante affair was certainly an indication of internal disagreements – but the leadership of the Cuban Revolution remained convinced of Soviet solidarity. More important, Che and Raúl Castro, in particular, were ideologically committed to the Soviet model and were surrounded by people who reinforced that belief. Had he chosen to, Che could easily have seen the contradictions in Eastern Europe – the economic unevenness (that he had commented on), the absence of democracy, the imperial ambitions of the Soviets, and the privations and hardships suffered by millions of Soviet and Chinese citizens. But he did not – until October.

In the Soviet Union, Khrushchev and others were drawing their own political conclusions from the missile crisis. It was argued it had demonstrated a new possibility of 'peaceful coexistence' between the US and the Soviets. Yet only a few weeks earlier Khrushchev had reassured Che of his commitment to the Latin American revolution. For Che this was anathema. How could a revolutionary anti-imperialist ever accept peaceful negotiation with the enemy! In Moscow voices were raised that expressed a growing suspicion of Guevara. In the dispute between Russia and China, they argued, Che had been too close to the Chinese.

Until now, Che had not expressed any public disagreement with the Russians. But he had often expressed his anger and irritation at the inadequacy of Russian goods, and at the inefficiency and unreliability of their economy. After all, for Che everything rested on the ability of the Cubans to industrialise at speed. If he thought the Russians would help to achieve that, or indeed could do so, he was quickly having to acknowledge his mistake. Within Cuba, too, Che was scathing about what he saw as a lackadaisical attitude displayed by the Communists. The influence of the old PSP on Fidel and the Cuban state had simply created a larger bureaucracy, and a more complex and sometimes corrupt political structure. It had not produced the changes Che hoped for.

At the same time Che had maintained his relationships with the guerrilla groups elsewhere in the region. Through most of 1962 he had been working with a group of Argentines led by Jorge Masetti, preparing to set up a guerrilla operation in his own country, as well as with others in Bolivia, Peru and Central America. Che recognised that an isolated Cuba could not survive and, unlike Castro, felt that the relationship with the Russians would now represent an intolerable compromise.

The revolution must spread. A series of Latin American countries with anti-imperialist or socialist governments would perhaps provide an environment in which Cuba could survive and gain access to the raw materials and oil it needed without depending on the Russians or the US. And within Cuba a different culture – a society convinced that moral incentives like solidarity and self-sacrifice were worth far more than bonuses or access to consumer goods – could guarantee rapid economic progress. This would be helped by a system in which the whole economy could function as a single unit without competition or profits:

> There was no longer any doubt that his and Fidel's paths had begun to diverge. Fidel's goal was to consolidate Cuba's economic wellbeing and his own political survival, and for that he was willing to compromise. Che's mission was to spread the socialist revolution. The time for leaving Cuba was drawing near.[118]

It would still be two years before he left, but Che's mind was increasingly turning to the revolution beyond Cuba. At the same time, many of his speeches and writings of early 1963 recognise the increasingly fragile state of the Cuban economy. His economic hopes had come to little. Indeed, some within the Cuban state argued that Guevara's relentless centralising of policy and his single-minded dedication to industrial development were responsible for the crisis, at least in part. By now, the lack of spare parts was becoming critical, and Eastern

European replacements were proving useless. Improvisation kept the cars and buses going and the machines turning. In government circles, and within the state machine, Che was becoming less popular. Among the population, however, his star remained as high as ever.

There were signs that the political tensions were also having psychological consequences. He was putting on weight, and although he ascribed this to the cortisone he was taking for his asthma, the reality was that his sedentary lifestyle was taking its toll. His wild hair was shorter and neater – though he still refused to wear his olive green uniform in the regulation way, with his shirt neatly tucked under his belt. Che had become a government minister spending many hours a day in meetings and committees. In those early months of 1963 he had very little time to spend with his newly born daughter Celia. As their family grew (Che had four children now), Aleida had little opportunity to spend time with her husband. He spent more and more time at the ministry as things became fraught, and the crises and difficulties more frequent and intense. The murmurings against him were becoming persistent too, and his mood reflected the tension. Che, for all his easy manner, was always a harsh disciplinarian – although always most relentlessly with himself. Now, he was prone to quite angry outbursts of frustration with those around him.

For Che the issue of voluntary labour was now absolutely central. His argument had been that revolutionaries do not work for material rewards, but out of conviction. Work for the general good should never be a sacrifice, but the expression of selflessness and socialist consciousness – that was the essence of the 'new man'. As he said to a colleague, 'I'm not interested in an economic transformation unless it's accompanied by a socialist morality'.[119] Voluntary labour, therefore, was exemplary, the expression of the highest level of political understanding. That was why it was expected of every revolutionary, and why Che threw himself into voluntary labour in the early months of the year.

There is an air of desperation about Che in this period. The changes he had hoped for had not materialised. The fraternal support of the Soviet Union fell apart at the first challenge. The centralised control he had fought to establish had failed to operate as he had hoped. An essay written in February 1963, 'Against bureaucracy',[120] was in some ways a self-criticism as well as an exposé of the inefficiencies and shortcomings of the Cuban state. The insistence on voluntary labour as a solution reflected this characteristic of Che's thinking from the very outset, the conviction that the will and determination of revolutionaries could overcome all obstacles, even objective ones. But this idealism was now openly criticised by the old Communists around Fidel.

In May Che made a speech at the anniversary commemoration of the magazine *Hoy* which was closely echoed in his prologue to a trite and dogmatic book on the Marxist-Leninist party – an anthology of quotes from Soviet theorists and speeches by Fidel:

> One of his biographers, Massari, laments Che's 'praise for this wretched, theoretically weak little book'. It is an odd thing that Che, who was so critical of the economic path taken by the Soviets, seemed to have barely any understanding of the social disaster, the authoritarianism and the repressive nature of Soviet society. The reality is that he did not have the theoretical instruments which would have allowed him to distance himself from them. He was locked in a primitive Marxism.[121]

This may seem a harsh judgement, yet it is borne out in the debates that were to follow. The journal *Nuestra Industria* (*Our Industry*) began publication in June, with the clear purpose of initiating a debate about the future of the Cuban economy. Here Che developed his ideas about an economy based on moral (ie political) rather than material incentives, continuing the theme of the creation of the 'new man'. The pro-Soviets in and around government entered into the argument with ferocity, but Che gave no quarter.

At the same time he was conducting another argument with Communists in Latin America. With all the authority of the Cuban Revolution behind him, Guevara insisted that revolutionary struggle must be armed struggle based on the peasantry – with material and political support offered to any group prepared to launch guerrilla warfare on that basis, whatever their political origins. Thus, for example, he supported Trotskyist groups in Venezuela among others – to the fury of Cuba's Communist allies.

In a postscript to his *Guerrilla Warfare*, published in September, Che reiterated the ideas set out in his original work:

> To be the vanguard party is to be at the head of the working class in the struggle for power, to know how to guide it towards seizure of that power, even leading it through short cuts.[122]

While he uses the term 'working class', Che emphasises over and over again in his essay that the guerrilla army must be located in the countryside, and recruit above all among the peasantry, because it is they who have suffered the most brutal exploitation. But suffering, of course, does not create revolutionaries. On the contrary, without collective organisation and the confidence that comes from the experience of struggle, and without the power to strike at the very heart of capitalism – the machinery of production – suffering can produce despair and a sense of impotence.

In fact, the article is a veiled attack on the Communist parties of Latin America, who had signally failed to lead a revolution. Che was right to level that accusation against them. Yet in rejecting their specific role he was also jettisoning a tradition of mass revolutionary organisation and substituting for it the determined actions of a small group of revolutionaries who could, in his words, 'provoke the enemy's fury'. Experience would soon show that this fury would be directed at the mass of working people rather than the guerrillas themselves. And the dominance of a guerrilla theory, in which the mass of workers were reduced to a passive, supporting role, left them organisationally and politically unprepared for those assaults.

The timing of the article was highly significant. While the economic argument was developing with growing ferocity, Fidel was moving towards the position that Che was defending. Despite his rapturous reception on a visit to Moscow in March, Fidel was also recognising the necessity of an international movement to help Cuba to break out of its political and economic isolation.

Quoting repeatedly from Fidel's January 1962 Second Declaration of Havana, Che repeated that the next phase of revolution must be Latin American:

> As Fidel stated, the *cordilleras* of the Andes will be the Sierra Maestra of Latin America... This means that it will be a protracted war; it will have many fronts and it will cost much blood and countless sacrifices for a long period of time.[123]

Che will have had in mind the guerrilla unit that was already preparing to launch perhaps the first of these war fronts – in Salta, Argentina. It would provide, in the following year, tragic and terrible lessons about the limits of the strategy.

In the same month Che returned to Moscow at the head of a Cuban government delegation for the anniversary celebrations of the Russian Revolution and to attend the opening of a 'Soviet-Cuban Friendship House' in Moscow. His reception was very different from the one he had received three years earlier – Che's attitude to the Soviet Union had also changed profoundly. The Latin American Communist parties about to meet in regional congress in Havana had complained bitterly to Moscow about the new political positions of Che and Fidel. After the missile crisis, the policy of Communist parties across the world followed Moscow's line of 'peaceful coexistence'. Historically, these parties had always followed the political direction set out by the Soviet Union.[124] The message delivered to Che during his visit was unmistakable. The guerrilla war policy was an unacceptable challenge to the strategy of gradual change.

Returning to Cuba, Che made a speech on 30 November in which he made clear he had been unimpressed by his Moscow conversations. It was significant that he delivered his speech in Santiago, well away from the Communist Party congress that was taking place at the same time in Havana.

> Though few people realised it, Che's no-show at the Havana conference was the first sign that something fundamental had shifted. For anyone who cared to notice, Che was already in the process of extracting himself from his normal routine and would soon vanish from their midst.[125]

According to Anderson, Che told Fidel that he wanted to leave the government at around the same time.

13 | **Neither marriage nor divorce**

The parting of the ways would not come for another year, but the decision was taken at the end of 1963.[126] Che's attention was turning to Africa, and in his September speech he spoke at length about the situation there. He had visited Algeria briefly in July and established some rapport with Ben Bella, president of the country and leader of its armed liberation struggle. They agreed that recent events in the Congo placed it at the heart of the continent. The murder of Patrice Lumumba in 1961 had eliminated one of the most inspiring leaders of the African liberation process, but in 1963 the struggle was about to erupt again, under the leadership of some of Lumumba's closest aides.

In Latin America the Argentine guerrilla organisation Che had supported and organised from Cuba was now established in Salta province, making ready for the beginning of its campaign early in 1964. It is almost certain that Che had intended to lead the group – two of his closest collaborators were already with Masetti. In Che's mind his home country was always the key, and there was a whole network of organisations there which could create a powerful force if they could be persuaded to unite behind him. Bolivia and Venezuela were also important in Che's thinking, although the Venezuelan Communist Party was implacably opposed to any armed operation in the country, and even the Bolivians had given only formal endorsement to Che's general strategy.[127]

These were the issues drawing Che back to the struggle. His fits of anger and his increasingly trenchant attitudes towards those around him were indications of his deepening frustration. Although he had a family that he loved, Che's sense of his historic role was probably not to be achieved from behind a desk.

There were other factors pushing him too. His growing unpopularity with the Communists close to Fidel, and with the Soviets, was one. Just a few months earlier he had enjoyed an authority in the Cuban Revolution second only to Fidel's. Now it seemed Fidel was drifting away from him, perhaps even seeing him as a rival.

There were elements of Castro's conduct which Che found unacceptable. In one sense Che was dogmatic, a believer in unbreakable principles and absolute beliefs. Fidel, by contrast, was a consummate politician, a pragmatist who made decisions in the light of circumstances, and changed them as the situation changed. While enjoying the adoration of the Russian crowds, for example, Fidel was simultaneously exploring avenues of communication with the United States. And there was some movement, until the Kennedy assassination put an abrupt end to the secret talks. Che knew of these approaches and disapproved of them violently. From the beginning of the revolution he had argued that imperialism was the enemy and that it could never change – only the defeat of imperialism could open the path to revolution. In this, Che was absolutely consistent.

Towards the end of the year, however, Fidel began to speak publicly of a return to armed struggle on the Latin American continent. Che was distrustful of what he saw as rhetoric designed only to impress both the US and the Soviet Union. Indeed, the signing of new agreements with the Russians signalled to him, correctly, that the bonds were growing tighter. This came as no surprise, of course. What had appeared to be highly technical debates about the economy conducted in the second half of 1963 were in fact extremely political. The moral/material incentives controversy was really about whether the economy would be organised around ideas of profitability and efficiency or around social need.[128] In later official accounts this dispute has been described as a difference of degree – for Che it was a difference of politics and principle.

Many of Che's colleagues argued with him when his decision to leave became known early in 1964, urging him to stay and fight for the policies of industrialisation he had argued for. But Che was adamant. As far as he was concerned, the Cuban-Soviet Sugar Agreement of 1964 only confirmed what he already knew. The Cuban economy would once again rest on sugar production, with all the implications of dependency on the external market that this entailed. The creation in July of a separate Department for Sugar Production which fell outside his control was the final proof, if proof were needed.[129]

Che was preparing his return to the guerrilla struggle. Some writers have suggested this was simply the result of his congenital restlessness, combined with the feeling that his work in Cuba was done. It is a romantic account, and profoundly misleading. Che was a revolutionary, devoted to the political project of liberation. It is impossible to ignore the fact that his star was fading, his authority in the revolution diminishing by the day. He had made his criticisms of the Communists in Moscow and Latin America clear, and now they were marginalising him in a systematic way.

This is not to say Che had no intention of returning to the armed struggle. But the reasons for that return were complex and, above all, political. However, his plans did not follow the anticipated course. The People's Guerrilla Army in Argentina, which he had intended to lead, was destroyed and the majority of its membership killed before it was able to embark on any actions. By the end of March 1964 it had ceased to exist.

For now, Argentina was not a serious possibility. Congo had figured in Che's thinking for many months and would now loom larger still. Che's place in the Cuban Revolution and in the new Cuban state was losing significance. He was more involved in preparing the next phase of his life. In March he headed the Cuban delegation to a UN conference on trade and development in Geneva. The rapturous welcome he received when he rose to speak was evidence enough of his continuing status and popularity abroad. Perhaps it marked the moment when Che's role and stature began to separate from his relationship with Cuba. His speech was short and fiercely anti-imperialist – it seemed almost a prelude for his more famous address to the UN in New York later in the year. And while he was cheered by some, he was also cold-shouldered by many Eastern European and Latin American delegates.

He took a few days to visit Algeria again, and to review the African situation with Ben Bella. What he heard confirmed his conviction that Congo was a key front in the worldwide struggle against imperialism. This was clearly in his mind when he returned to Cuba in April. But he was still in charge of the industrial ministry. His exasperation at meetings and discussions grew deeper. At one meeting he pulled out a series of new products – a doll, a zip that didn't work, toys that fell apart – and threw them on the table to illustrate what was wrong with the nascent Cuban industry. Eastern European machines were crude and mediocre, and work was done in slapdash ways.

Che also seemed willing to comment, at least in private, on other issues of concern. He noted the consolidation in power of the new ruling bureaucracy. In an interview with a Mexican journalist he discussed the role of the trade unions as simple 'transmission belts' from government – their supposed independence was a sham.[130] He continued to debate the big questions about the shape and nature of a socialist economy, but to his colleagues he seemed increasingly bored and listless, remote from the more pressing day to day issues.

In November Che returned to the anniversary celebrations in Moscow. It was an entirely diplomatic visit. In an informal discussion with Cuban students in Havana he described his trip, but set out again his criticisms of the East European Communist countries. Their insistence on letting the laws of the market determine the shape of the economy had held back their development, he said, and put them at a deepening disadvantage in relation to the capitalist countries of the West. It was his last but one contribution to the debate that had absorbed him for over two years, and which he had lost.

His attendance at the UN General Assembly in New York on 9 December was in a way his last act as a Cuban and his first as an international revolutionary. His speech was uncompromising. He denounced imperialism in the strongest terms and made critical comments about the Communist bloc, albeit obliquely. Much of his speech was concerned with Congo, which suggested to many commentators that he was seeking new directions. He hinted as much in a TV *Face the Nation* special in which he was interviewed by three journalists. It emerged many years later that he also met an American senator and later presidential candidate, Eugene McCarthy, and confirmed Havana's support for revolutionary movements in Latin America.[131]

In January Che returned to Algeria. There, in an interview with the widow of the great anti-imperialist writer Frantz Fanon, Guevara said, 'Africa is one or perhaps the most important battlefield today... There are huge possibilities for success here in Africa, due to the existing unrest, but there are also great dangers'.[132] He spent a few days in China in early February before travelling through several African countries to meet what he called (in English) the 'freedom fighters' of the continent. A private account of those meetings, published 30 years after his death, suggests that he was concerned at their high lifestyle and general lack of preparation.[133]

On 25 February Che gave a widely publicised and highly controversial speech in Algiers at a conference on Third World solidarity. It was the most explicit and far-reaching criticism of the Soviet Union he had yet delivered. He said the failure to support liberation movements made the Russians 'accomplices of imperialism', and he demanded that the 'socialist' countries provide material support for the liberation fighters in Vietnam and Congo. The Russians were furious. Was Fidel in agreement with Che? It continues to be a matter of debate. But Fidel was at the airport to meet Che when he returned in mid-March. They talked in private, a conversation that lasted several hours and was unrecorded. It's likely Fidel was happy Che had thrown down a gauntlet to the Russians without implicating him. At the same time it guaranteed Che could never hold an official position again in a Cuban government that continued to deal with those he had offended.

When Che came back to Cuba he had already resigned. It has been suggested that he was then persuaded to go to Congo, even though Latin America was the focus of all Che's strategic thinking. In fact there were few hopeful signs in Latin America at this juncture, and Che himself had placed Congo at the heart of the anti-imperialist struggle. He said his farewells to Aleida and a new son, Ernesto, who was only a few days old. On 1 April a clean-shaven man in a suit, wearing heavy glasses, slipped through Havana's international airport. There were no ceremonies to mark Che Guevara's last farewell to Cuba.

Che's best known essay, 'Man and Socialism in Cuba', was published in the radical Uruguayan journal *Marcha* in March 1965, and only later in Cuba, in the army magazine *Verde Olivo*. In one sense it summarised the debates and arguments of the previous four years. Why did he lay such emphasis on the question of a new consciousness? It was certainly not for economic reasons, or because committed people are more efficient producers – although the debates about moral incentives did reflect what he saw as the urgent need to transform Cuba's economy at speed. It went to the very heart of Che's political ideas, for it emphasised the subjective over the objective, the effort of will that could overcome unpromising material conditions. This was a central notion in his *Guerrilla Warfare*, and was restated with even more fervour in his later article 'Guerrilla Warfare: A Method'. It flew in the face of a revolutionary tradition which recognised the dialectical relationship between the individual and his or her circumstances that Marx had summarised in a famous dictum: 'Men make

history but not in circumstances of their own choosing.'
Che preferred to ignore the second part of Marx's thoughts
and emphasise only the vision of new and different social
relationships:

> Man under socialism, despite his apparent standardisa-
> tion, is more complete; despite the lack of perfect
> machinery for it, his opportunities for expressing himself
> and making himself felt in the social organism are infi-
> nitely greater.[134]

For Che, the new society is born of a spiritual transformation, hence the stern critique of dogmatism in the arts:

> This is not a matter of how many pounds of meat one
> might be able to eat, nor of how many times a year some-
> one can go to the beach... What is really involved is that
> the individual feels more complete, with much more
> internal richness and much more responsibility.[135]

For Marx, the possibility of social transformation arises
out of the development of the productive forces which
clash, under capitalism, with the social relationships on
which that development depends. A growing capacity for
producing wealth together with a deepening inequality
between those who own and those who produce that
wealth – that is the defining characteristic of capitalism. It
is also the reason why capitalism produces class struggle.
The outcome of that struggle, however, is in no sense
inevitable – success for the working class will rest on its
organisation, its leadership, and the ideas that drive its
struggle forward. The crucial thing, however, is that a revolution is made by a whole class, the working class, exercis-
ing its power as a class.

Che's impatience, his emphasis on the consciousness and conviction of the revolutionaries, arose out of a belief, as he says repeatedly, that the change need not wait upon the construction of that organisation but can come later. It is the revolutionaries, and not the working class, who are the key actors in his conception of revolution.

Che wrote this article as he was travelling to the Congo. He had left behind another, much shorter piece – a letter of farewell to Fidel. But this would not see the light for another six months. He had left Cuba behind now. Though he expected to rejoin the struggle in Argentina, it was Congo that beckoned. That was due in part to the collapse of the Argentine guerrillas. Yet it was consistent with Che's vision of how to defeat imperialism that the struggle should be fought on several fronts. The war in Vietnam was intensifying, and Che never doubted that Latin America would be a second front of resistance, even though the situation at this point was discouraging. The Guatemalan and Peruvian guerrillas had suffered serious setbacks, and no base had been built in either Bolivia or Argentina.

The resurgence of resistance struggles in Congo in the previous year suggested to him that a third front was already in operation. Che was part of a small advance group. In the course of the year about 100 Cubans would journey there. Che had been in Africa just two months earlier. His brief visit to China in early February had presumably been undertaken to assess the Chinese government's attitude to the struggle in Congo. Now he travelled through several countries to Dar es Salaam in Tanzania, whose president, Julius Nyerere, was an unconditional supporter of Cuba. Che had already expressed his reservations about some of the leaders of the African resistance – he found them ill-prepared, confused and lazy. Now some of the key leaders of the Congolese struggle were not there to meet the Cubans or their mysterious leader 'Ramon' (Che's nom de guerre). They were in Cairo engaged in lengthy internal arguments and disputes.

On 24 April Che crossed Lake Tanganyika from the Tanzanian port of Kigame and stood for the first time on Congolese soil. What he found, in contrast to his expectations, was a divided and undisciplined force deeply resentful of leaders who spent most of their time living a life of luxury well away from the fighting.[136]

Che was shocked. He also had great difficulties communicating with the fighters, although a French-speaking interpreter had come with him. Anderson reports his concern at the strength of magical thinking in the area.[137] More important, the Cubans had not researched the terrain sufficiently. Their jungle training, for example, had not prepared them for the canyons, escarpments and cliffs in this mountainous region.

The geographical and political importance of Congo was undeniable. But the situation in this vast country was enormously complicated. The mineral-rich Katanga region seceded under Moise Tshombe in mid-1964, with Western encouragement. Tshombe assembled a mercenary force under British colonel Mike Hoare which was waging an organised and well-supplied war against the rebels. It was clear that his British, Belgian and North American supporters saw this 'independent' Katanga as a bridgehead from which to re-establish control over Congo as a whole.

By the middle of the year it was the leftist, nationalist rebels who controlled the majority of this enormous territory. However, they were far from united. Several contending armed groups vied for power, despite their notional allegiance to a united National Liberation Council. The situation was further complicated by the support given to rival groups by China and Russia, whose division of the

Communist world was now reproduced in every country where there was Communist organisation.

Western intervention later in 1964, and the push against the rebels led by Katanga's mercenary Hoare, changed the balance of forces. The first direct encounter between Hoare and the Liberation Council forces took place at the important hydroelectric plant at Bendera in June, soon after the arrival of the Cubans. It was a rout and Hoare was the victor. Guevara's diary records his frustration. But he also reveals an extraordinary lack of preparation, of knowledge of the terrain and of the political realities. Once again, Che had ignored the objective conditions in his conviction that subjective factors were paramount.

In fact, by the time Guevara's group reached Congo the situation had changed profoundly from a year earlier. The internal divisions were intensifying. The leader in whom Guevara had been led to place the greatest confidence, Laurent Kabila, proved far less competent than he had imagined. As if that was not enough, Che and many of those around him were sick with malaria – and Guevara's asthma was severe.

The central government of Congo, for its part, was seeking to negotiate with Tshombe. Then in that same month of June – the first in which the Cubans had been actively engaged in combat – Ben Bella, Cuba's principal ally in the region, was overthrown in Algeria. Guevara wrote in his diary entry summing up the month, 'The disorganisation is total.' Tshombe's mercenaries and Western assistance to the central government at Leopoldville (now Kisangani), combined with the disorganisation and incompetence of the rebel armies, were slowly destroying the insurrectionary forces.

In October, the Congolese president Kasavubu ousted Tshombe. He then attended a meeting of African governments to announce the end of the secession and the withdrawal of white mercenaries. In return he asked those gathered to end their support for the rebels. Even Nyerere agreed. The Congo rebellion was at an end. On 20 November 1965 Guevara and the rest of the Cuban fighters rowed back across the lake to Tanzania.

The expedition to Congo had been a disaster. The words of Egyptian leader Nasser to Guevara earlier that year must have come back to haunt him. Nasser had warned him, 'Another Tarzan, a white man among black men, leading and protecting them... It can't be done'.[138]

Why did Che choose to go to the Congo? Some have suggested he saw it as a training opportunity for a future core of Cuban guerrilla fighters. Che himself said, 'I shall go to the Congo because it is the hottest spot in the world now... I think we can hurt the imperialists at the core of their interests in Katanga'.[139] That might have been true a year earlier, but by the time Che arrived imperialism had organised its response and was carrying it through with particular ruthlessness. The Congolese rebels were untrained, internally divided and undisciplined. Perhaps Che imagined his reputation and status could unify the rebel forces, or that his military knowledge could overcome their disadvantages. If so, it was naive or arrogant. In any event, the debacle was evidence that general principles are not enough – the particular circumstances of a struggle shape its character.

It is true that Che's expedition was supported by Fidel. In part, this is explained by the systematic misinformation Castro was receiving about the reality of the Congolese situation. It is true that Cuba was active in Africa from then on, and particularly in Angola and the Horn of Africa in the 1970s. But by then the Cuban role was intimately connected with Soviet interests in the region. This was especially true in Ethiopia, where Cuban soldiers fought the

Somali insurrection in defence of a repressive, authoritarian regime which was an ally of the Soviets. It may be true that similar considerations had an influence on the decision to send a Cuban force to Congo.

Six months after his secret departure from Cuba, in October 1965, Fidel published Che's famous letter of farewell, in which he resigned his government posts and his Cuban citizenship:

> I carry to new battlefields the faith that you instilled in me, the revolutionary spirit of my people, the feeling of fulfilling the most sacred of duties: to fight against imperialism wherever it may be… I will just say that I free Cuba of any responsibility except that which stems from my example.[140]

It was a paean of praise to Fidel. It was also a document which removed any responsibility from Fidel or the Cuban state for anything that might happen in Africa. But the question remains – why did Fidel choose to make the letter public when he did? It caused Che great difficulties with his Cuban comrades, to whom it smacked of betrayal. It also made it impossible for Che to return to Cuba except in secret and in silence.

Che stayed for a while in Dar es Salaam before travelling to Prague. It was there, in discussion with comrades from Cuba, that he decided to take the struggle to Bolivia. There is some argument as to why he chose Bolivia.[141] But it is widely agreed that those 12 or so weeks in the Czech capital were the darkest in Che's life. He was unwell, and made sicker by an out of date Russian cough remedy. He was also alone. Aleida did visit him, but their relationship had already been strained to breaking point before he left for Congo. He was beset by advice and pressures, but his future was undecided.

Che Guevara, 1964   Osvaldo Salas

14 | **A final journey**

The final decision may well have been jointly taken by Fidel and Manuel Piñeiro, the head of the Cuban security services. Che himself wanted to return to Argentina, but his allies were dead or in prison. The Venezuelan guerrillas were established, but riven with internal disputes and, for complicated reasons, opposed to Che coming. The Peruvian guerrillas had suffered a recent and crushing defeat.

The discussions in Prague finally settled on Bolivia, where Masetti's guerrillas had gathered in preparation for their incursion in 1964. Demoralised after Congo, and feeling marginalised and neglected as a result of Fidel's publication of his farewell letter, the vindication of the Argentine guerrilla strategy must have been at the centre of Che's mind. In that sense, Bolivia was little more than a staging post for the reconstruction of a guerrilla *foco* in the north of Argentina. To organise it from a small worker's flat in central Prague, of course, made little sense. But Che was extremely reluctant to return to Havana, and it took a visit from Ramiro Valdés, an old comrade and one of

Cuba's most powerful officials, to persuade him to return incognito to the Cuban capital and there begin the organisation of the guerrilla force.

Ernesto Che Guevara returned to Cuba in mid-July 1966. There were no welcoming committees. Instead he went straight to an isolated estate to begin the training of his Bolivian group. Some were Cuban, some Bolivian students. He was accompanied everywhere by the sinister Piñeiro, now one of Fidel's most intimate associates.

Whether the Bolivian enterprise had Castro's personal seal of approval remains unclear. Che had returned to Cuba with no great enthusiasm, but accepted that Cuba was a better base of organisation than Eastern Europe. Fidel attested later that Che was extremely impatient – implying that his preparations were rushed and incomplete.[142] Nonetheless, Che remained there until November while his emissaries laid the groundwork for his arrival.

Was it an ill-advised enterprise? Why was Che so adamant that the Bolivian guerrillas should be established as quickly as possible? Was it because he felt a pressing need to vindicate his vision after the Congo disaster – or because he still felt certain that the historical moment was particularly favourable for the struggle against imperialism? Undoubtedly there was an element of both of these. He might also have been influenced by the tone of Fidel's recent speeches, which had raised again the banner of Latin American revolution despite the disapproval of Moscow. Fidel was preparing for a Tricontinental Conference in January 1967 and tilting his public pronouncements towards the liberation fighters of the Third World. Perhaps it was also a way of opening a small space of independence from both Russia and China. Looking back, it seems clear that this did not represent any serious change of direction on Castro's part. If anything, it was a tactical shift, the sort of pragmatic adaptation at which Fidel was so expert. While he gave Che's project material support, at no time did he give it his public approval. From Che's point of view, however, this offered a possibility of vindicating his strategy. He was, after all, an internationally renowned revolutionary who just 18 months earlier had enjoyed acclaim wherever he went.

Had there been other options available, Che might have reflected that Bolivia was not the best place from which to launch a general Latin American guerrilla offensive.[143] A few months earlier Peru had seemed a far more promising launch pad, but by the end of 1966 the leaders of both major Peruvian guerrilla organisations were dead and their people dispersed. Perhaps Bolivia was fixed in Che's thoughts as a staging post and a rearguard base for the Argentine guerrilla army which was still his first priority.

Fidel subsequently maintained that Bolivia had been his suggestion. But Che was wedded to the guerrilla strategy – and its failures in Argentina, Peru and Guatemala seem to have reinforced that conviction rather than called it into question. In one sense, Bolivia might have seemed a suitable place for the building of a revolutionary movement. In 1952 a revolution led and carried through by a movement led by the working class had imposed a left nationalist government under the National Revolutionary Movement (MNR) led by Víctor Paz Estenssoro. It nationalised the country's main export earner – the tin mines. For reasons that are complex, this high point of popular struggle was followed by a series of compromises and betrayals. By the early 1960s the miners' union and the national trade union federation (the COB) were once again locked in struggle with the state.

In 1964 Paz Estenssoro – once again president – was ousted by a military coup led by airforce officer René

Barrientos. Two years later, Barrientos became president. The situation was complicated. Bolivia is a country divided in two by geography. The High Andes and the vast mountain plateau of the *altiplano* are the source of Bolivia's mineral wealth and home to the Aymara-speaking indigenous communities who have for centuries provided the labour for the deep shafts. But to the east lie the fertile valleys and rainforest areas around Cochabamba and Camiri, the centre of the oil-producing region.

Bolivia's extraordinary history of mass struggle and resistance was born out of the mining communities. After his coup in 1964, Barrientos focused all his repressive energy on these leaders of the working class. A year of terrible repression was followed by the consolidation of his power and the almost complete suppression of workers' organisation. But Barrientos had popular support in the eastern part of the country, for he had pledged to continue (albeit selectively) the agrarian reform of the previous three or four years which had given more than 200,000 peasants their own plots of land. These were not the land-starved peasantry who Guevara argued would form the backbone of a guerrilla army. On the contrary, their attitudes were conservative and suspicious of revolutionary activity, particularly if it was conducted by foreigners. Yet it was in this region that Che elected to establish his first guerrilla *foco*, at Ñancahuazú – on the opposite side of the country from the heartland of Bolivia's glorious revolutionary tradition.

The peasants were unlikely to support the guerrillas. The key revolutionary force in the country was rooted in a very different part of the country and was momentarily disorganised. Furthermore, the terrain was very different from the ideal location Che had suggested in *Guerrilla*

Warfare. And elsewhere in Latin America there had been a series of setbacks for the strategy. The objective conditions were very unpromising.

Yet at the Tricontinental Conference in Havana in January of that year, Fidel seemed to re-adopt the perspective of the Latin American revolution, distancing himself from the gradualist programmes of the region's official Communist parties. And the secretary of Bolivia's Communist Party, Mario Monje, had spent some time in Havana and assured Castro of his support for armed struggle. The support never materialised, and was a prime reason for the failure of Che's Bolivian guerrillas. But Monje's betrayal should have surprised no one who knew the political situation in Bolivia at the time.

The Bolivian Communist Party had divided like every other in the wake of the Russia-China split. Those who adopted the Chinese position (Maoism) criticised the Soviet pursuit of peaceful coexistence with the West and supported an idea of rural armed struggle. The main Bolivian Maoist party, the PCML, was formed in 1965. Its leader, Oscar Zamora, went to Cuba the following year and offered Che logistical support. This could have been significant, since the criticisms of the Communist Party's collusion with the nationalist government had won over a number of important trade union leaders, and in particular some leading miners. But while Castro was content for Zamora to be in Havana, his dealings were exclusively with Monje and the Bolivian Communists. Monje's offer to support armed struggle, flying in the face of Communist policy in the rest of the region, must be seen as an attempt to outmanoeuvre Zamora rather than a sincere change of direction.

The Tricontinental Conference had listened to a message from Che. It was his last public declaration and perhaps his most famous. It began with a famous quotation from José Martí, leader of Cuba's 19th century independence movement and the greatest of its 19th century poets:

> Now is the hour of the furnaces, and only light should be seen.[144]

But the phrase which resonated across the world, as US imperialism intensified its war against Vietnam and backed repressive responses to liberation movements across the world, was Che's invocation to 'create one, two, three, many Vietnams'. Perhaps, in the end, that was the central impulse behind his Bolivian project – to create the first of many anti-imperialist fronts. He was now clear that while capitalism existed the struggle could not end, and he offered 'our lives, our sacrifice' as an inspiration for the struggles to come. Yet it is hard to believe he anticipated that the sacrifice would come so soon.

15 October 1966 was set for the departure of Che and his team. An observer reported the last conversation between Che and Fidel, although he could only see what was happening from a distance.

> Castro did the talking, while Che was sullen and withdrawn; Castro was vehement, Che quiet. At last Fidel ran through all the problems, both inherent and circumstantial, in the Bolivian expedition. He emphasised the lack of communications, Monje's hesitations, the organisational weakness of Inti and Coco Peredo. He intended to dissuade Guevara, or at least induce him to postpone his trip… Fidel's gestures revealed his desperation at Che's stubbornness. They sat down again for a long while, in silence. Then Fidel got up and left. Che was overtaken by impatience, for the last time in his life.[145]

Che was impatient because he knew that the fragile project was starting to unravel. His contact in La Paz, his lifelong and devoted collaborator Harry 'Pombo' Villegas, had already communicated his concern about the operation in late September.[146] So had Régis Debray, a postgraduate from the Sorbonne in Paris whose *Revolution in the Revolution*[147] generalised Che's ideas for a global audience. Debray was particularly favoured by Fidel. For reasons which, to this writer at least, are hard to fathom, Debray had been asked to analyse the general situation in Bolivia and advise Che. In fact Debray was not enthusiastic about the Bolivian *foco*, even though he was a zealous advocate of the theory, which is presumably why Fidel too was blowing cold. But Che was obdurate.

Pombo's messages suggest that there were still misunderstandings with Monje and the Bolivian Communists. Pombo and Debray were in contact with the Maoists around Zamora among others, and were resistant to breaking those links. But it would soon emerge that the claims coming from all sides were inflated, and there were several agendas at work at the same time.

Of the three possible sites for the first guerrilla base, Che chose the village of Ñancahuazú:

It would have been harder to find in all Bolivia an area less well suited to the fighting of a guerrilla war, especially by the *foco* method... The area was one of broken hill chains, complex river systems and deep ravines; it offered good cover but was extraordinarily difficult to traverse and had no defensible perimeter... [It] was very sparsely populated and the peasants living there held land in adequate quantities, were highly parochial in outlook...and had never demonstrated any deep-seated discontent or proclivity for radical politics.[148]

The only explanation for the choice is that this site was the closest to the Argentine border and Che was really not particularly concerned with the situation in Bolivia itself. Yet from a different political perspective Bolivia would have been a key locus of struggle. It had a long tradition of courageous and sustained working-class struggle, it had a high level of union organisation and deeply rooted revolutionary traditions. The heart of that tradition was in the highlands, around the mines and the city of La Paz. This was not an ideal moment for a major offensive, but it would have been a perfect time for the patient rebuilding of political organisation, especially with the enormous moral authority of Che behind it. Guevara, however, was wedded to the idea of guerrilla warfare, and did not see the organised working class as a central actor in his vision of revolution.

Che reached Bolivia towards the end of October, crossing the border from Brazil. At Ñancahuazú preparations were under way. In December, Mario Monje arrived, accompanied by Tania (Tamara Bunke), the East German interpreter whom Che had met on his travels in Europe in 1960.

Che's diary records that meeting on 31 December, and it uncovers Monje's real motives. Monje offered to resign from the party in order to take over the leadership of the guerrillas. He also insisted he must conduct relations with other political organisations in Latin America. On this point Che was resolute:

> Under no circumstances would I accept his second point. I was the military leader and there was no more to discuss on that. The discussion got stuck on this point and from then on we just went round in circles.[149]

The relationship between the Bolivian Communist Party and Che's guerrilla band effectively ended that night. Monje was discredited with his own party leadership – it was never clear to what extent he was speaking for them anyway – and while it continued to support Che in theory, in practice it blocked any attempt by party members to help him. The Maoists, for their part, were high on rhetoric but low on achievement. A small group of miners did arrive eventually, but they were a small splinter group under Moisés Guevara, an ex miners' leader. It was clear that the promised Bolivian recruits were not going to materialise. Supplies were short and several of the company were in the camp for reasons that were less political than mercenary. The portents were grim.

In January Che organised the guerrillas into three groups for a training exercise. Four men remained behind, while the rest embarked on an expedition. It was supposed to last for a few days. Instead, it was six weeks before they returned, exhausted and undernourished, having lost their way several times, battled with rushing rivers and suffered plagues of mosquitoes. Three comrades had drowned. Che had lost eight kilos in weight and looked hollow-eyed and emaciated. His state of mind was not helped by what he found on his return to the camp on 19 March.

The activity around the farm had attracted the unwelcome attention of local peasants. So many arrivals and departures were almost bound to awake suspicion. The army had been informed and raided two days earlier. They discovered the diary of one of the Cubans and sketches of members of the group, including Che. On 23 March, the guerrillas and the army met in combat for the first time. Seven soldiers were killed and the rest of the patrol captured. But within a week or so the camp was taken and the guerrillas were on the move.

The *foco* was not ready to begin operations in any sense –

they had not been able to take all their supplies, and their training was certainly inadequate. From now on the 40 guerrillas were in permanent retreat from a military force of some 1,500. Just before the flight from the camp, two new visitors had arrived – the Argentine artist Ciro Bustos and the ubiquitous Régis Debray. It was clear they would have to be sent out of the area, which obliged Che to split the tiny force in two. One group would move south and take the visitors to safety – in fact they were picked up as soon as they left the group. Debray's arrest was international news and brought the harsh light of publicity to the guerrillas. The town of Camiri received some unexpected visitors in subsequent days, including the publishers Feltrinelli (from Italy) and François Maspéro (from France) and leading Trotskyist Tariq Ali (from Britain).

In the unforgiving terrain, the guerrillas were now separated and out of touch. Che wrote in his diary entry summarising the month of April:

> We are completely isolated. Several comrades are ill, which has forced us to divide our group, which has greatly weakened us; the peasant base has failed to develop, although the repression will at least achieve the neutrality of most of them. Their support will come later. No one has joined and apart from two deaths, we have lost Loro, who disappeared after the Taperillas action.[150]

By June Che's asthma, combined with the shortage of medicines and increasing hunger, meant he could only move from place to place on a donkey. Yet while the guerrillas were engaging in their cat and mouse game with the army, the miners again took their place at the heart of Bolivian politics. In late April a new movement began, followed by demonstrations throughout the Andean region.

On the night of 23-24 June, the feast day of San Juan (St John), the army massacred miners and their families gathered for a meeting in the mining camp of Llallagua. Shock and rage took hold of the country. Thirty thousand attended the funeral of the murdered delegates and their families, despite the army occupation of the area, and the miners launched a general strike that would last for two weeks.

Some days later, the guerrillas issued their 'Communiqué Number 5 to the Miners of Bolivia'.[151] It is an extraordinary document – in many ways arrogant, unrealistic and profoundly revealing of how distant Che's ideas were from the self-emancipation of the working class:

> We are now recovering from a defeat caused by a repetition of tactical errors on the part of the working class. We are patiently preparing the country for a deep-going social revolution that will transform the system from top to bottom.[152]

This was from an isolated and sick group of fewer than 20. Very soon they would be all who were left. In August the other group, led by the Cuban Joaquín, was ambushed and all were killed, although Che had no idea when he passed the very spot where it had happened a few hours later. In September just 17 guerillas were left and they split into several groups.

On 8 October Che was captured by the army. Crippled by asthma for which his medication had run out, Che was being carried along the steep sides of the ravine called Quebrada del Yuro on the back of a young miner. Twenty four hours later he was dead, murdered in the village schoolroom of La Higuera by the Bolivian army under the watchful eye of US military advisers. Only five guerrillas survived – three Cubans, including Pombo, who crossed into Chile, and two Bolivians.

> The defeat of Che's guerrilla operation and the main flaw in Che's strategy – as well as Debray's theorising about revolutionary guerrilla warfare in *Revolution in the Revolution* stem from might be called a kind of military vanguardism. By reducing popular revolution to a special form of guerrilla warfare, Che's strategy and Debray's early writings overemphasised the military aspects of initiating a revolutionary struggle against an unjust regime. And they underemphasised the political dimension of organising the base of popular support needed for a successful revolutionary struggle.[153]

Bolivia illustrates in vivid colour the consequences of the separation of the military and the political, of the revolutionaries from the working class. In Havana's Museum of the Revolution a special room is set aside to commemorate the Bolivian experience of Guevara. It is described as heroic, epic and exemplary. However, it does Che's memory no credit to refuse to acknowledge the brutal truth that this was a terrible and costly failure born of Che's insistence that the will of the revolutionary can overcome objective conditions and substitute the individual for the movement of an entire class. That way lies martyrdom, not social revolution.

15 | **Death and resurrection**

Then as now, the face of Che Guevara was a symbol of revolutionary hope. His death, while it sanctified him, yielded political lessons that few at the time were prepared to learn. The picture of his haggard face and naked torso on the schoolroom table in Bolivia flew around the world. It was, after all, the eve of the 1968, the year of rebellion.[154]

In Cuba, 1968 was named after Che – the 'Year of the Heroic Guerrilla'. The dead hero became a living myth. The prominence of Che's image served to identify the Cuban Revolution with the movements of 1968, and to suggest that Cuba was still central to a global revolutionary movement.

It was also at this time that, taking advantage of the wave of sympathy towards a small country alone and heroically confronting aggression, Castro convened a Congress of Intellectuals at the end of 1967; few of the delegates seemed to realise that what they were applauding was

already sliding into the past… And in 1968 the posters of
Che in which he appears as a slightly hippyish apostle
begin to appear.[155]

Che's image served to emphasise the collective ideology of a Cuban Revolution still demanding material sacrifices from its population. The moral certainty of Fidel's
rhetoric exactly paralleled the economic insecurity of a
revolution under siege. But then Che himself had laid the
ground for that merging of his image and the Cuban state.
In some ways, especially in his last writings, Che had
expressed something like reverence for Castro. Now Castro used Che as a myth to justify himself and to symbolise
his final attempts to maintain some independence from
the Soviet Union.

The sugar harvest of 1969-70 (the *Gran Zafra*) was to be
the final attempt at a great economic leap out of dependency. The whole society was mobilised to the sugar fields
in the name of the voluntary labour and self-sacrificing
socialist consciousness that Che had advocated. It was a
major harvest – but it was far from producing the ten million tons that could have yielded the kind of surplus that
might have allowed investment in new industrial sectors of
the economy. By 1970 Castro was reconciled to Cuba's
integration into the Russian sphere of influence. In the following decade Cuba's presence in Africa was shaped and
determined by Soviet foreign policy objectives – despite
the rhetoric of selfless solidarity that accompanied the
movements of Cuban troops. On the island itself, a decent
basic standard of living was combined with the progressive
abandonment of any aspiration to economic independence. The promise of democracy was postponed indefi-
nitely as power became concentrated in the small group at
the head of the state, the party and the army.[156]

As the emphasis on will and the revolutionary spirit gave way to a limited internal differentiation – between workers, and between bureaucrats and workers, for example – the revolutionary utopianism of Guevara seemed less and less relevant, and the memory of Che ceased to occupy the central place in the revolution's pantheon of heroes. It was to resume its iconic status, however, when Cuba found itself face to face with disaster in the wake of the withdrawal of Eastern European support in 1986, and the collapse of the entire Communist bloc in 1989. Castro knew there was severe economic scarcity to come, and that in times of crisis the masses would no longer tolerate the corruption, the wealth of some and the poverty of many. And there was no justification for the absence of any kind of authentic democracy when the capacity to act in defence of their own interests was the only weapon that Cuban workers could employ against the forces of the market.

For Castro, the issue was survival – his own, and that of a Cuban state still facing a ruthless US economic embargo. To this end, he initiated the process he called 'rectification', and called forth again the ghost of his comrade from the days of the Sierra:

Che Guevara symbolised the values guiding the 'rectification process'. Newspaper articles as well as books appeared on Che…In a speech marking the twentieth year since Guevara's death, Castro commented that the country was rectifying all that was a negation of Che's ideas, Che's style and Che's spirit. Castro mentioned that Cubans were to rectify those things – and there were many – that strayed from the revolutionary spirit, revolutionary work, revolutionary virtue, revolutionary effort and revolutionary responsibility.[157]

Quotations from Che on massive billboards lined the major highways and were draped from public buildings in Havana. Che's selflessness, his vision of a different future and his incorruptibility were exploited to veil the reality of a society entering a competitive global market at a disadvantage which could only be counterbalanced by more material sacrifices by the mass of its people. Yet there were those who were growing quickly and visibly richer as a result of the process.

Here then was the irony. This symbol of struggle and revolutionary integrity was harnessed by an authoritarian regime which had been responsible for the very errors now so vehemently denounced in Che's name. For those in Cuba who have lived the reality of 50 years of revolution, these calls for sacrifice must seem hollow, as they wait for hours in queues for the cattle trucks that pass for buses while they are passed in the streets by the Mercedeses and Toyotas of the new rich.

Yet beyond Cuba, the image of Che has been reborn or rediscovered by a new generation desperate to create a better, more humane, more just and equal world. Che expresses their denunciation of exploitation and war. Che is their promise of a better world to come.

There are some, of course, who sell the face as mere style – as an image without a history, without a complex and contradictory life. These are the commodity-makers who will co-opt any and every expression of the human spirit and make it into a product for immediate consumption. Che has been their victim too.

But the millions who wear the T-shirt that bears Che's face, or the scarf of the Zapatistas, or the beret with the red star, are making a different kind of statement. In the words of the anti-capitalist movement, it is that 'a better world is possible'. The image of Che does not belong to a state, any state, but to the movement that has rediscovered him. The revolutionary consciousness that he enshrines is not a religious spirit – the revolution does not need saints, but fighters whose life, whose errors and misjudgements, are as much a part of their legacy as the symbols they leave behind.

Revolutions, after all, are made by human beings who take from the past the practical lessons, for good and ill, that will help them to understand and exercise their own collective power to build a socialist world.

The 100,000-strong D14 demonstration in Brussels in 2001: 'Another Europe is possible' Jess Hurd www.reportdigital.co.uk

Notes

1 See Tony Cliff, *State Capitalism in Russia* (London: Bookmarks, 1996).

2 See Tom Hayden (ed), *The Zapatista Reader* (New York: Thunders Mouth Press/Nation Books, 2002).

3 John Lee Anderson, *Che Guevara: A Revolutionary Life* (London: Bantam Press, 1997), p21.

4 Paco Ignacio Taibo II, *Ernesto Guevara, También Conocido Como El Che* (Mexico: Joaquín Mortiz, 1996), p27.

5 And he was right – see Uki Goñi, *The Real Odessa* (London: Granta Books, 2002).

6 See Che's father's book – Ernesto Guevara Lynch, *Mi Hijo el Che* (Havana: Arte y Literatura, 1988). See also Pierre Kalfon, *Che: Ernesto Guevara, Une Légende du Siècle* (Paris: Éditions du Seuil, 1997), pp39-41.

7 See Anderson, pp24-25, 30-31.

8 For an insightful analysis of Peronism see Daniel James, *Resistance and Integration: Peronism and the Argentine Working Class* (Cambridge: Cambridge University Press, 1988).

9   See the piece by Communist Party leader Vittorio Codovilla in M Lowy, *Marxism in Latin America* (New Jersey: Humanities Press, 1992), pp83-86.

10 Jorge Castañeda, *Compañero* (London: Bloomsbury, 1997), p33.

11 Kalfon, p61.

12 Che's account of this journey is in Che Guevara, *The Motorcycle Diaries* (London: Fourth Estate, 1996). See also Alberto Granado, *Con el Che Guevara* (Córdoba, 1995).

13 Quoted in Anderson, p62.

14 See F Diego García and Oscar Sola, *Che: Images of a Revolutionary* (London: Pluto Press, 1997), pp30-31.

15 Taibo, p41ff.

16 As Jean Cormier does in his *Che Guevara* (Paris: Gallimard, 1996), and as is echoed to some extent in Matilde Sánchez's narrative in *Che: Images of a Revolutionary*.

17 On the Bolivian revolution, see James Dunkerley, *Rebellion in the Veins* (London: Verso, 1984). On the place of minerals in Latin America's history see Eduardo Galeano, *Open Veins of Latin America* (London: Latin America Bureau, 1997), and Domitila Barrios de Chungara's extraordinary account of her life in the mining communities, *Let Me Speak* (London: Stage 1, 1978).

18 Che Guevara, *Back on the Road* (New York: Grove Press, 2002), pp17-18.

19 Castañeda, p64.

20 Anderson, p123.

21 'As an Afterthought', in *The Motorcycle Diaries*, pp150-152.

22 See Stephen Schlesinger and Stephen Kinzer, *Bitter Fruit* (New York: Anchor, 1983). On the role of the US in Central America generally see Jenny Pearce's brilliant *Under the Eagle* (London: Latin America Bureau, 1981).

23 See Anderson, pp122-123; and Michel Lowy, *Marxism in Latin America*, pp113-124.

24 Castañeda, p72.

25 Castañeda, p67.

26 *Back on the Road*, p67.

27 *Back on the Road*, p67.

28 *Back on the Road*, pp78-79.

29 *Back on the Road*, p79.

30 Quoted in Anderson, p165.

31 Claudia Lightfoot, *Havana* (London: Latin America Bureau, 2002), p40.

32 On the sugar issue see René Dumont, *Cuba: Socialism and Development* (New York: Grove Press, 1970); Arthur Mc-Ewan, *Revolution and Economic Development in Cuba* (London, 1981). See also James O'Connor, *Origins of Socialism in Cuba* (New York: Cornell University Press, 1970).

33 Ken Loach's film *Land and Freedom* illustrates this conflict brilliantly. For a contemporary account see Felix Morrow's *Revolution and Counter-Revolution in Spain* (New York: Pathfinder, 1974).

34 See K S Karol, *Guerrillas in Power* (London: Jonathan Cape, 1971), pp81-98.

35 Mario Vargas Llosa has recently given us an exhaustive and chilling portrait of Trujillo in his novel *The Feast of the Goat* (London: Faber & Faber, 2001).

36 Fidel Castro, *History Will Absolve Me* (London: Jonathan Cape, 1968).

37 Anderson, p173.

38 Taibo, p93.

39 Castañeda, p85.

40 Lee Lockwood, *Castro's Cuba, Cuba's Fidel* (New York: Macmillan, 1967), pp143-144.

41 The crushing of the Hungarian workers' uprising in 1956 and the split between Russia and China in 1962 were key turning points.

42 Anderson, p178.

43 They did sign an agreement in Mexico in September 1956, according to Taibo, p119.

44 Castañeda and Hugh Thomas in *The Cuban Revolution* (London: Weidenfeld & Nicolson, 1986) among them.

45 See E Bayo, *Mi Aporte a la Revolución Cubana* (Havana: Imp Ejército Rebelde, 1960).

46 Taibo, pp107-110.

47 Taibo, p109.

48 Taibo, p115.

49 In this, as in so many other things, Anderson provides an alibi for Fidel: 'Whatever the provenance of the money Fidel continued to act as his own man' (Anderson, p204). Presumably that would also be true, in his view, when Fidel began to receive CIA money, as Tad Szulc confirms in his biography of Fidel, *Fidel: A Critical Portrait* (New York: Monthly Review Press, 1986). This seems to me to be a very questionable assertion, and a pretty glib explanation. At worst, it suggests that Fidel took money from anyone. At best, it presents Castro as a wholly opportunist politician.

50 From Che Guevara, *Reminiscences of the Cuban Revolutionary War* (New York: Monthly Review Press, 1998). These diaries were published in Havana in 1963. But according to Anderson (p213) they were a 'carefully censored' version of Che's actual field diary – without the acerbic comments he made about some of his comrades who later became leading figures in Cuba after the revolution.

51 Carlos Franqui, *The Twelve* (New York: Lyle Stuart, 1968). Originally called *El Libro de los Doce*.

52 Che Guevara, *Guerrilla Warfare* (New York: Monthly Review Press, 1961).

53 Anderson, p231.

54 Anderson, p233.

55   There was, however, a small group of active trade unionists in Guantánamo, some of them Trotskyists, who worked with M-26-J. See Gary Tennant, 'The Hidden Pearl of the Caribbean: Trotskyism in Cuba', *Revolutionary History*, vol 7, no 3 (London: Porcupine Press, 2000), particularly pp175-183.

56   Quoted in Anderson, p245.

57   His connections made Smith a rather compromised US representative in Batista's final months, so he was replaced. He makes his feelings about the liberal takeover of US policy towards Cuba very clear in his memoir *The Fourth Floor* (New York: Random House, 1962). (The title refers to the fourth floor of the State Department, where the relevant desk was to be found.)

58   Che Guevara, *Episodes of the Cuban Guerrilla War* (New York: Pathfinder, 1996), p129.

59   The pain of his loss never left her – it might have been one reason for her suicide over 20 years later.

60   See Anderson, p235.

61   Kalfon, p197. Franqui wrote the definitive history of the guerrilla struggle, *El Libro de los Doce*, but he would later become disillusioned with Fidel's concentration of power in his own hands and become one of his fiercest critics. See his *Family Portrait With Fidel* (New York: Random House, 1985).

62   John Gerassi (ed), *Veneceremos: Speeches and Writings of Ernesto Che Guevara* (London: Weidenfeld and Nicolson, 1968), p75.

63   Anderson, pp280-281.

64   The doubts he expressed and the criticisms he voiced did not subsequently appear in the edited version of those diaries published in Havana in 1963.

65   For a very different perspective on this period see Gary Tennant, 'The Hidden Pearl of the Caribbean: Trotskyism in Cuba'.

68 Che's summary of the year is in *Episodes*, pp260-276.

69 *Episodes*, p267.

70 See p53 above.

71 *Episodes*, p273.

72 Quoted in Anderson, p319. See 'A Decisive Meeting' in *Episodes*, pp316-322.

73 See Kalfon, p212.

74 As Earl T Smith complained in *The Fourth Floor*. Smith had originally been sent to haul Batista over the coals – but Smith's anti-Communism was stronger than his diplomatic obligations, and he became a vocal supporter of the dictator.

75 Anderson, p324.

76 Castañeda, p122.

77 Kalfon, p223.

78 Taibo, p275.

79 One obvious sign of this was the fact that Raúl Castro, who was the closest of the leadership to the PSP, was kept then and thereafter very much in the shadows.

80 This is contentious of course. Pierre Kalfon, for example, says that 'Castro was doing Che a favour', giving him time to adjust (p239).

81 Anderson, p376.

82 Reinaldo Arenas, whose autobiography *Before Night Falls* (originally published in 1992) would later represent one of the most powerful indictments of sexual and political repression in Cuba, described the euphoria and abandon of those early days, which he experienced as a young teenager discovering his own sexuality at the same time as the revolution was testing its own festive personality.

83 Camilo Cienfuegos, who had been chosen to lead the victorious procession to Havana, was killed in a still unexplained air crash in October. A popular figure, he was never central to the revolution's political mythology – and he certainly came from a very different political background from

Che or Fidel. After his death, Camilo continued to be acknowledged for his military role – yet he seems curiously absent from the iconography of the revolution.

84 It would later become the province of the man they called 'Redbeard', Manuel Piñeiro, witchfinder-general of the new society.

85 C Wright Mills, *Listen, Yankee* (New York: Ballantine, 1960).

86 Robert Scheer and Maurice Zeitlin, *Cuba: An American Tragedy* (New York, 1963).

87 *Guerrilla Warfare*, p15. See also Michel Lowy, 'Revolutionary Warfare', in *The Marxism of Che Guevara* (New York/London: Monthly Review Press, 1973), pp75-112.

88 Karl Marx and Frederick Engels, *The German Ideology* (Moscow, 1964), p86.

89 An example of where that perspective can lead is in Jean Stubbs's discussion of the role of Fidel Castro in the revolution in her *Cuba: The Test of Time* (London: Latin America Bureau, 1989), in which she develops all sorts of arguments to show that Castro's popularity is sufficient justification for his years in unelected power.

90 Castañeda, p147.

91 For further examples see Régis Debray's 1965 article 'Latin America: The Long March', in *New Left Review* 33 (July-September 1965), pp17-58.

92 This discussion may be found in detailed form in René Dumont, *Cuba: Socialism and Development* (New York: Grove Press, 1970). My thanks to Chris Harman for setting out the issues, as well as for his thorough and helpful reading of the first draft of this book.

93 From the speech Guevara made in January 1959 , 'Social Projections of the Rebel Army', quoted in Castañeda, p152.

94 Castellanos describes the event in Hilda Barrio and Gareth Jenkins, *The Che Handbook* (London: MG, 2003). pp162-164.

95 Taibo, p360.

96 Kalfon (p270) quotes from a letter written to his mother during his mission in which he says just that 'I have very much in my mind the sense of historic duty'.

97 Anderson, p468.

98 While there are a number of detailed studies of this period from both sides of the divide, there are few works that penetrate so deeply into the paranoid psyche of US government, the Miami mafia and the Kennedy clique as James Ellroy's *The Cold Six Thousand* (London: Century, 2001), a brilliant thriller in the 'noir' tradition.

99 The title of a speech he made on 18 June 1960, reprinted in Gerassi (ed), pp144-167.

100 The debates and discussions among socialists on these issues have produced an enormous literature. In the revolutionary socialist tradition Tony Cliff's *State Capitalism in Russia* and Nigel Harris's *The Mandate of Heaven: Marx and Mao in Modern China* (London: Quartet, 1978) are crucial entry points into these questions.

101 Castañeda (p178) quotes this as part of a group of documents in which Che set out the reasons for the founding of the labour camps – a term attended in itself by a terrible legacy, the memory of Stalin's labour camps in which dissidents and accidental victims alike died in their thousands in the 1930s. As Castañeda points out in his footnote, these documents were and remain suppressed, and do not appear in any collections of Che's writings. Anderson, for his part, addresses Guanacahabibes only later in his account, and almost as an aside (p567).

102 Reinaldo Arenas's autobiography *Before Night Falls* gives a sense of the atmosphere at the time and the persecutions that followed from the perspective of a gay writer. Julian Schnabel's film of the book includes some extracts from *PM*. See also Ian Lumsden, *Machos, Maricones and Gays* (Philadelphia: Temple University Press, 1996).

103 It is important to say, nonetheless, that Cuban literacy rates before 1959 were in fact among the highest in the region. Which does not detract from the campaign's achievements.

104 See Kalfon, pp305-306. The official delegate from Cuba was Aníbal Escalante, who would very soon find himself in a Cuban jail, accused of leading a dissident faction against Castro.

105 Kalfon, p305.

106 K S Karol's *Guerrillas in Power* provides the fullest background to Cuban relationships with the Communist bloc. One brief encounter on his journey, however, would have an unexpected impact on Che's future life. In East Germany his interpreter was a young woman called Tamara Bunke. A year later she came to Havana at the invitation of Armando Hart, though he indiscreetly suggested he had done so on Che's behalf. All that is certain is that she would join him again in Bolivia six years later.

107 Kalfon, p307; Anderson, p495.

108 For the details, fictionalised but extremely well informed, see James Ellroy, *The Cold Six Thousand*.

109 US ambassador to the UN Adlai Stevenson was not informed of the operation and indignantly insisted that these were Cuban planes. It later emerged that they had taken off from Nicaragua that morning.

110 More recent publications and writings have confirmed the impact of the defeat in the United States – and Kalfon (p316) argues that it led directly to the escalating US intervention in Vietnam and elsewhere.

111 Anderson, p523.

112 Taibo, p413.

113 It was only much later, when the Russians abandoned Cuba in 1986, that Fidel would speak openly and with derision about the industrial goods Cuba received from Eastern Europe.

114 For a full account of the Cuban missile crisis see Laurence Chang and Peter Kornbluh (eds), *The Cuban Missile Crisis* (New York: New Press, 1992); K S Karol's *Guerrillas in Power*, pp249-281; and of course Oliver Stone's film *Thirteen Days*.

115 Castañeda, p229.

116 I sat through most of the night before with three friends, listening to the Voice of America and talking about how we wanted to spend our last day on earth. It may seem foolish now, but we were a generation raised under the cloud of a nuclear threat that shaped and inhabited our dreams.

117 Castañeda, p228.

118 Anderson, p587.

119 See Kalfon, pp362-375.

120 In Gerassi (ed), pp220-226.

121 Taibo, p468.

122 From 'Guerrilla Warfare: A Method', in Gerassi (ed), p269.

123 In Gerassi (ed), p275.

124 Until the Sino-Soviet split of 1962, that is, when for some groups Beijing replaced Moscow as the capital of world Communism.

125 Anderson, p616.

126 Castañeda (p249) describes the meeting between Che and Carlos Franqui in Paris that year. Franqui, author of a key history of the guerrilla struggle, had become estranged from Fidel and Che, and worked in Paris. But Franqui was a friend of Ben Bella, and that provided the opportunity for the two men to meet again. He recalled, 'Che was seeking another path. He considered the Cuban situation very difficult.' Other close friends and colleagues of Guevara are quoted in support of that view.

127 Nevertheless, as would become clear later, that formal agreement played a key role in Che's later decision to establish the Bolivian guerrilla army.

128 This is a simple and schematic attempt to sum up a very complex debate. There are more detailed analyses in Castañeda, pp255-263, and Bette Ann Evans, *The Moral Versus Material Incentives Controversy in Cuba* (Pittsburgh: University of Pittsburgh, 1973).

129 Even though the person put in charge of that department was one of his closest collaborators.

130 Taibo, pp492-493. It should be noted, however, that Che agreed that the unions should function as part of the state.

131 The papers were only released in 1994 and are discussed by Castañeda, p274.

132 Taibo, p512.

133 See Anderson, p621.

134 Che Guevara, *Man and Socialism in Cuba* (New York: Pathfinder Press, 1978), p12.

135 *Man and Socialism*, p20.

136 Che's African diary is published as Che Guevara, *The African Dream* (London: Harvill Panther, 2000).

137 Anderson, p641. Given the enduring influence in Cuba of *santería*, magical-religious ideas of African origin, it is surprising that he should have reacted so dramatically.

138 Richard Gott, in his introduction to *The African Dream*, pxxiii.

139 Gott, pxxiii.

140 Barrio and Jenkins, pp314-316.

141 See Anderson, pp680-682.

142 Kalfon, p474.

143 For the best available account of the contemporary history of Bolivia see James Dunkerley, *Rebellion in the Veins: Political Struggle in Bolivia 1952-82* (London: Verso, 1984).

144 The phrase 'La hora de los hornos' ('The hour of the furnaces') arose again as the title of an outstanding film made by the Perónist resistance to new military dictatorship in Argentina, which began with the Onganía coup in 1966. Military rule lasted until 1973 and then returned again with

extreme ferocity between 1976 and 1983, when 30,000 men, women and children were actively 'disappeared' in pursuit of 'Christian civilisation and social peace'.

145 Castañeda, pp344-345. The Peredo brothers, both Communists, were key to the whole enterprise. Fidel's judgement, however, was probably correct.

146 See Pombo's message for 24 September and the 28 September entry in Pombo Villegas, *A Man of Che's Guerrilla 1966-68* (New York: Pathfinder Press, 1997), pp109-111.

147 Régis Debray, *Revolution in the Revolution* (Harmondsworth: Penguin, 1969).

148 James Dunkerley, p140.

149 *El Diario del Che en Bolivia* (Havana, 1968), pp46-47. The diary has been republished many times since – but this is a definitive version. The dates, of course, do not vary from edition to edition.

150 *Diario del Che*, p171.

151 Reproduced in Villegas, pp204-206.

152 Villegas, p205.

153 Richard L Harris, *Death of a Revolutionary: Che Guevara's Last Mission* (New York/London: Norton, 2000), p252.

154 I am sure that those of us who gathered in the central square of Essex University to mourn Che's death were not alone. Nor were we the only student revolutionaries who decorated our walls with his portrait as we prepared to demonstrate against the US war in Vietnam.

155 François Maspero, 'Introduction', Janette Habel, *Ruptures à Cuba* (Paris: La Breche, 1989), p23.

156 I have developed the more general analysis of the Cuban Revolution elsewhere. See 'Can Castro Survive?', in *International Socialism* 56 (Autumn 1992), p83. See too Habel.

157 Susan Eckstein, *Back From the Future* (New Jersey: Princeton, 1994), p62.

Bookmarks Publications Ltd is linked to an international grouping of socialist organisations:

Australia International Socialist Organisation, PO Box A338, Sydney South.

Austria Linkswende, Postfach 87, 1108 Wien.

Britain Socialist Workers Party, PO Box 82, London E3 3LH. www.swp.org.uk

Canada International Socialists, PO Box 339, Station E, Toronto, Ontario M6H 4E3.

Cyprus Ergatiki Demokratia, PO Box 27280, Nicosia.

Czech Republic Socialisticka Solidarita, PO Box 1002, 11121 Praha 1.

Denmark Internationale Socialister, PO Box 5113, 8100 Aarhus C.

Finland Sosialistiliitto, PL 288, 00171 Helsinki.

France Socialisme par en bas, BP 15-94111, Arcueil Cedex.

Germany Linksruck, Postfach 44 0346, 12003 Berlin.

Ghana International Socialist Organisation, PO Box TF202, Trade Fair, Labadi, Accra.

Greece Sosialistiko Ergatiko Komma, c/o Workers Solidarity, PO Box 8161, Athens 100 10.

Holland Internationale Socialisten, PO Box 92025, 1090AA Amsterdam.

Ireland Socialist Workers Party, PO Box 1648, Dublin 8.

Italy Comunismo dal Basso, Leeder, CP Bologna, Succ 5.

New Zealand Socialist Workers Organisation, PO Box 13-685, Auckland.

Norway Internasjonale Socialisterr, Postboks 9226, Grønland, 0134 Oslo.

Poland Pracownicza Demokracja, PO Box 12, 01-900 Warszawa 118.

Spain En Lucha, Apartado 563, 08080 Barcelona.

Uruguay Izquierda Revolucionaria.

Zimbabwe International Socialist Organisation, PO Box 6758, Harare.